C-3471   CAREER EXAMINATION SERIES

This is your
PASSBOOK for...

Senior Account Clerk-Typist

Test Preparation Study Guide
Questions & Answers

NATIONAL LEARNING CORPORATION®

COPYRIGHT NOTICE

This book is SOLELY intended for, is sold ONLY to, and its use is RESTRICTED to individual, bona fide applicants or candidates who qualify by virtue of having seriously filed applications for appropriate license, certificate, professional and/or promotional advancement, higher school matriculation, scholarship, or other legitimate requirements of education and/or governmental authorities.

This book is NOT intended for use, class instruction, tutoring, training, duplication, copying, reprinting, excerption, or adaptation, etc., by:

1) Other publishers
2) Proprietors and/or Instructors of "Coaching" and/or Preparatory Courses
3) Personnel and/or Training Divisions of commercial, industrial, and governmental organizations
4) Schools, colleges, or universities and/or their departments and staffs, including teachers and other personnel
5) Testing Agencies or Bureaus
6) Study groups which seek by the purchase of a single volume to copy and/or duplicate and/or adapt this material for use by the group as a whole without having purchased individual volumes for each of the members of the group
7) Et al.

Such persons would be in violation of appropriate Federal and State statutes.

PROVISION OF LICENSING AGREEMENTS – Recognized educational, commercial, industrial, and governmental institutions and organizations, and others legitimately engaged in educational pursuits, including training, testing, and measurement activities, may address request for a licensing agreement to the copyright owners, who will determine whether, and under what conditions, including fees and charges, the materials in this book may be used them. In other words, a licensing facility exists for the legitimate use of the material in this book on other than an individual basis. However, it is asseverated and affirmed here that the material in this book CANNOT be used without the receipt of the express permission of such a licensing agreement from the Publishers. Inquiries re licensing should be addressed to the company, attention rights and permissions department.

All rights reserved, including the right of reproduction in whole or in part, in any form or by any means, electronic or mechanical, including photocopying, recording, or by any information storage and retrieval system, without permission in writing from the Publisher.

Copyright © 2024 by
National Learning Corporation

212 Michael Drive, Syosset, NY 11791
(516) 921-8888 • www.passbooks.com
E-mail: info@passbooks.com

PUBLISHED IN THE UNITED STATES OF AMERICA

PASSBOOK® SERIES

THE *PASSBOOK® SERIES* has been created to prepare applicants and candidates for the ultimate academic battlefield – the examination room.

At some time in our lives, each and every one of us may be required to take an examination – for validation, matriculation, admission, qualification, registration, certification, or licensure.

Based on the assumption that every applicant or candidate has met the basic formal educational standards, has taken the required number of courses, and read the necessary texts, the *PASSBOOK® SERIES* furnishes the one special preparation which may assure passing with confidence, instead of failing with insecurity. Examination questions – together with answers – are furnished as the basic vehicle for study so that the mysteries of the examination and its compounding difficulties may be eliminated or diminished by a sure method.

This book is meant to help you pass your examination provided that you qualify and are serious in your objective.

The entire field is reviewed through the huge store of content information which is succinctly presented through a provocative and challenging approach – the question-and-answer method.

A climate of success is established by furnishing the correct answers at the end of each test.

You soon learn to recognize types of questions, forms of questions, and patterns of questioning. You may even begin to anticipate expected outcomes.

You perceive that many questions are repeated or adapted so that you can gain acute insights, which may enable you to score many sure points.

You learn how to confront new questions, or types of questions, and to attack them confidently and work out the correct answers.

You note objectives and emphases, and recognize pitfalls and dangers, so that you may make positive educational adjustments.

Moreover, you are kept fully informed in relation to new concepts, methods, practices, and directions in the field.

You discover that you are actually taking the examination all the time: you are preparing for the examination by "taking" an examination, not by reading extraneous and/or supererogatory textbooks.

In short, this PASSBOOK®, used directedly, should be an important factor in helping you to pass your test.

SENIOR ACCOUNT CLERK-TYPIST

DUTIES
Maintains a complex set of financial records, compiles and prepares or assists a supervisor in preparing difficult and complex financial or statistical reports. May supervise a number of subordinate personnel engaged in maintaining departmental accounts and general books including cashbooks, voucher registers, general ledgers, appropriation ledgers, sales books and general journal; posts entries to these books from supporting records and prepares routine statements. In addition to the accounts work, performs difficult and responsible typing duties. Work may include utilization of computers or word processors with financial capabilities. Performs related work as required.

SCOPE OF THE EXAMINATION
The written test will be designed to test for knowledge, skills, and/or abilities in such areas as:
1. Fundamentals of accounting and bookkeeping;
2. Understanding and interpreting written material; and
3. Office record keeping.

HOW TO TAKE A TEST

I. YOU MUST PASS AN EXAMINATION

A. WHAT EVERY CANDIDATE SHOULD KNOW

Examination applicants often ask us for help in preparing for the written test. What can I study in advance? What kinds of questions will be asked? How will the test be given? How will the papers be graded?

As an applicant for a civil service examination, you may be wondering about some of these things. Our purpose here is to suggest effective methods of advance study and to describe civil service examinations.

Your chances for success on this examination can be increased if you know how to prepare. Those "pre-examination jitters" can be reduced if you know what to expect. You can even experience an adventure in good citizenship if you know why civil service exams are given.

B. WHY ARE CIVIL SERVICE EXAMINATIONS GIVEN?

Civil service examinations are important to you in two ways. As a citizen, you want public jobs filled by employees who know how to do their work. As a job seeker, you want a fair chance to compete for that job on an equal footing with other candidates. The best-known means of accomplishing this two-fold goal is the competitive examination.

Exams are widely publicized throughout the nation. They may be administered for jobs in federal, state, city, municipal, town or village governments or agencies.

Any citizen may apply, with some limitations, such as the age or residence of applicants. Your experience and education may be reviewed to see whether you meet the requirements for the particular examination. When these requirements exist, they are reasonable and applied consistently to all applicants. Thus, a competitive examination may cause you some uneasiness now, but it is your privilege and safeguard.

C. HOW ARE CIVIL SERVICE EXAMS DEVELOPED?

Examinations are carefully written by trained technicians who are specialists in the field known as "psychological measurement," in consultation with recognized authorities in the field of work that the test will cover. These experts recommend the subject matter areas or skills to be tested; only those knowledges or skills important to your success on the job are included. The most reliable books and source materials available are used as references. Together, the experts and technicians judge the difficulty level of the questions.

Test technicians know how to phrase questions so that the problem is clearly stated. Their ethics do not permit "trick" or "catch" questions. Questions may have been tried out on sample groups, or subjected to statistical analysis, to determine their usefulness.

Written tests are often used in combination with performance tests, ratings of training and experience, and oral interviews. All of these measures combine to form the best-known means of finding the right person for the right job.

II. HOW TO PASS THE WRITTEN TEST

A. NATURE OF THE EXAMINATION

To prepare intelligently for civil service examinations, you should know how they differ from school examinations you have taken. In school you were assigned certain definite pages to read or subjects to cover. The examination questions were quite detailed and usually emphasized memory. Civil service exams, on the other hand, try to discover your present ability to perform the duties of a position, plus your potentiality to learn these duties. In other words, a civil service exam attempts to predict how successful you will be. Questions cover such a broad area that they cannot be as minute and detailed as school exam questions.

In the public service similar kinds of work, or positions, are grouped together in one "class." This process is known as *position-classification*. All the positions in a class are paid according to the salary range for that class. One class title covers all of these positions, and they are all tested by the same examination.

B. FOUR BASIC STEPS

1) Study the announcement

How, then, can you know what subjects to study? Our best answer is: "Learn as much as possible about the class of positions for which you've applied." The exam will test the knowledge, skills and abilities needed to do the work.

Your most valuable source of information about the position you want is the official exam announcement. This announcement lists the training and experience qualifications. Check these standards and apply only if you come reasonably close to meeting them.

The brief description of the position in the examination announcement offers some clues to the subjects which will be tested. Think about the job itself. Review the duties in your mind. Can you perform them, or are there some in which you are rusty? Fill in the blank spots in your preparation.

Many jurisdictions preview the written test in the exam announcement by including a section called "Knowledge and Abilities Required," "Scope of the Examination," or some similar heading. Here you will find out specifically what fields will be tested.

2) Review your own background

Once you learn in general what the position is all about, and what you need to know to do the work, ask yourself which subjects you already know fairly well and which need improvement. You may wonder whether to concentrate on improving your strong areas or on building some background in your fields of weakness. When the announcement has specified "some knowledge" or "considerable knowledge," or has used adjectives like "beginning principles of…" or "advanced … methods," you can get a clue as to the number and difficulty of questions to be asked in any given field. More questions, and hence broader coverage, would be included for those subjects which are more important in the work. Now weigh your strengths and weaknesses against the job requirements and prepare accordingly.

3) Determine the level of the position

Another way to tell how intensively you should prepare is to understand the level of the job for which you are applying. Is it the entering level? In other words, is this the position in which beginners in a field of work are hired? Or is it an intermediate or advanced level? Sometimes this is indicated by such words as "Junior" or "Senior" in the class title. Other jurisdictions use Roman numerals to designate the level – Clerk I, Clerk II, for example. The word "Supervisor" sometimes appears in the title. If the level is not indicated by the title, check the description of duties. Will you be working under very close supervision, or will you have responsibility for independent decisions in this work?

4) Choose appropriate study materials

Now that you know the subjects to be examined and the relative amount of each subject to be covered, you can choose suitable study materials. For beginning level jobs, or even advanced ones, if you have a pronounced weakness in some aspect of your training, read a modern, standard textbook in that field. Be sure it is up to date and has general coverage. Such books are normally available at your library, and the librarian will be glad to help you locate one. For entry-level positions, questions of appropriate difficulty are chosen – neither highly advanced questions, nor those too simple. Such questions require careful thought but not advanced training.

If the position for which you are applying is technical or advanced, you will read more advanced, specialized material. If you are already familiar with the basic principles of your field, elementary textbooks would waste your time. Concentrate on advanced textbooks and technical periodicals. Think through the concepts and review difficult problems in your field.

These are all general sources. You can get more ideas on your own initiative, following these leads. For example, training manuals and publications of the government agency which employs workers in your field can be useful, particularly for technical and professional positions. A letter or visit to the government department involved may result in more specific study suggestions, and certainly will provide you with a more definite idea of the exact nature of the position you are seeking.

III. KINDS OF TESTS

Tests are used for purposes other than measuring knowledge and ability to perform specified duties. For some positions, it is equally important to test ability to make adjustments to new situations or to profit from training. In others, basic mental abilities not dependent on information are essential. Questions which test these things may not appear as pertinent to the duties of the position as those which test for knowledge and information. Yet they are often highly important parts of a fair examination. For very general questions, it is almost impossible to help you direct your study efforts. What we can do is to point out some of the more common of these general abilities needed in public service positions and describe some typical questions.

1) General information

Broad, general information has been found useful for predicting job success in some kinds of work. This is tested in a variety of ways, from vocabulary lists to questions about current events. Basic background in some field of work, such as sociology or economics, may be sampled in a group of questions. Often these are principles which have become familiar to most persons through exposure rather than through formal training. It is difficult to advise you how to study for these questions; being alert to the world around you is our best suggestion.

2) Verbal ability

An example of an ability needed in many positions is verbal or language ability. Verbal ability is, in brief, the ability to use and understand words. Vocabulary and grammar tests are typical measures of this ability. Reading comprehension or paragraph interpretation questions are common in many kinds of civil service tests. You are given a paragraph of written material and asked to find its central meaning.

3) Numerical ability

Number skills can be tested by the familiar arithmetic problem, by checking paired lists of numbers to see which are alike and which are different, or by interpreting charts and graphs. In the latter test, a graph may be printed in the test booklet which you are asked to use as the basis for answering questions.

4) Observation

A popular test for law-enforcement positions is the observation test. A picture is shown to you for several minutes, then taken away. Questions about the picture test your ability to observe both details and larger elements.

5) Following directions

In many positions in the public service, the employee must be able to carry out written instructions dependably and accurately. You may be given a chart with several columns, each column listing a variety of information. The questions require you to carry out directions involving the information given in the chart.

6) Skills and aptitudes

Performance tests effectively measure some manual skills and aptitudes. When the skill is one in which you are trained, such as typing or shorthand, you can practice. These tests are often very much like those given in business school or high school courses. For many of the other skills and aptitudes, however, no short-time preparation can be made. Skills and abilities natural to you or that you have developed throughout your lifetime are being tested.

Many of the general questions just described provide all the data needed to answer the questions and ask you to use your reasoning ability to find the answers. Your best preparation for these tests, as well as for tests of facts and ideas, is to be at your physical and mental best. You, no doubt, have your own methods of getting into an exam-taking mood and keeping "in shape." The next section lists some ideas on this subject.

IV. KINDS OF QUESTIONS

Only rarely is the "essay" question, which you answer in narrative form, used in civil service tests. Civil service tests are usually of the short-answer type. Full instructions for answering these questions will be given to you at the examination. But in case this is your first experience with short-answer questions and separate answer sheets, here is what you need to know:

1) Multiple-choice Questions

Most popular of the short-answer questions is the "multiple choice" or "best answer" question. It can be used, for example, to test for factual knowledge, ability to solve problems or judgment in meeting situations found at work.

A multiple-choice question is normally one of three types—
- It can begin with an incomplete statement followed by several possible endings. You are to find the one ending which *best* completes the statement, although some of the others may not be entirely wrong.
- It can also be a complete statement in the form of a question which is answered by choosing one of the statements listed.

- It can be in the form of a problem – again you select the best answer.

Here is an example of a multiple-choice question with a discussion which should give you some clues as to the method for choosing the right answer:

When an employee has a complaint about his assignment, the action which will *best* help him overcome his difficulty is to
- A. discuss his difficulty with his coworkers
- B. take the problem to the head of the organization
- C. take the problem to the person who gave him the assignment
- D. say nothing to anyone about his complaint

In answering this question, you should study each of the choices to find which is best. Consider choice "A" – Certainly an employee may discuss his complaint with fellow employees, but no change or improvement can result, and the complaint remains unresolved. Choice "B" is a poor choice since the head of the organization probably does not know what assignment you have been given, and taking your problem to him is known as "going over the head" of the supervisor. The supervisor, or person who made the assignment, is the person who can clarify it or correct any injustice. Choice "C" is, therefore, correct. To say nothing, as in choice "D," is unwise. Supervisors have and interest in knowing the problems employees are facing, and the employee is seeking a solution to his problem.

2) True/False Questions

The "true/false" or "right/wrong" form of question is sometimes used. Here a complete statement is given. Your job is to decide whether the statement is right or wrong.

SAMPLE: A roaming cell-phone call to a nearby city costs less than a non-roaming call to a distant city.

This statement is wrong, or false, since roaming calls are more expensive.

This is not a complete list of all possible question forms, although most of the others are variations of these common types. You will always get complete directions for answering questions. Be sure you understand *how* to mark your answers – ask questions until you do.

V. RECORDING YOUR ANSWERS

Computer terminals are used more and more today for many different kinds of exams.

For an examination with very few applicants, you may be told to record your answers in the test booklet itself. Separate answer sheets are much more common. If this separate answer sheet is to be scored by machine – and this is often the case – it is highly important that you mark your answers correctly in order to get credit.

An electronic scoring machine is often used in civil service offices because of the speed with which papers can be scored. Machine-scored answer sheets must be marked with a pencil, which will be given to you. This pencil has a high graphite content which responds to the electronic scoring machine. As a matter of fact, stray dots may register as answers, so do not let your pencil rest on the answer sheet while you are pondering the correct answer. Also, if your pencil lead breaks or is otherwise defective, ask for another.

Since the answer sheet will be dropped in a slot in the scoring machine, be careful not to bend the corners or get the paper crumpled.

The answer sheet normally has five vertical columns of numbers, with 30 numbers to a column. These numbers correspond to the question numbers in your test booklet. After each number, going across the page are four or five pairs of dotted lines. These short dotted lines have small letters or numbers above them. The first two pairs may also have a "T" or "F" above the letters. This indicates that the first two pairs only are to be used if the questions are of the true-false type. If the questions are multiple choice, disregard the "T" and "F" and pay attention only to the small letters or numbers.

Answer your questions in the manner of the sample that follows:

32. The largest city in the United States is
    A. Washington, D.C.
    B. New York City
    C. Chicago
    D. Detroit
    E. San Francisco

1) Choose the answer you think is best. (New York City is the largest, so "B" is correct.)
2) Find the row of dotted lines numbered the same as the question you are answering. (Find row number 32)
3) Find the pair of dotted lines corresponding to the answer. (Find the pair of lines under the mark "B.")
4) Make a solid black mark between the dotted lines.

VI. BEFORE THE TEST

Common sense will help you find procedures to follow to get ready for an examination. Too many of us, however, overlook these sensible measures. Indeed, nervousness and fatigue have been found to be the most serious reasons why applicants fail to do their best on civil service tests. Here is a list of reminders:

- Begin your preparation early – Don't wait until the last minute to go scurrying around for books and materials or to find out what the position is all about.
- Prepare continuously – An hour a night for a week is better than an all-night cram session. This has been definitely established. What is more, a night a week for a month will return better dividends than crowding your study into a shorter period of time.
- Locate the place of the exam – You have been sent a notice telling you when and where to report for the examination. If the location is in a different town or otherwise unfamiliar to you, it would be well to inquire the best route and learn something about the building.
- Relax the night before the test – Allow your mind to rest. Do not study at all that night. Plan some mild recreation or diversion; then go to bed early and get a good night's sleep.
- Get up early enough to make a leisurely trip to the place for the test – This way unforeseen events, traffic snarls, unfamiliar buildings, etc. will not upset you.
- Dress comfortably – A written test is not a fashion show. You will be known by number and not by name, so wear something comfortable.

- Leave excess paraphernalia at home – Shopping bags and odd bundles will get in your way. You need bring only the items mentioned in the official notice you received; usually everything you need is provided. Do not bring reference books to the exam. They will only confuse those last minutes and be taken away from you when in the test room.
- Arrive somewhat ahead of time – If because of transportation schedules you must get there very early, bring a newspaper or magazine to take your mind off yourself while waiting.
- Locate the examination room – When you have found the proper room, you will be directed to the seat or part of the room where you will sit. Sometimes you are given a sheet of instructions to read while you are waiting. Do not fill out any forms until you are told to do so; just read them and be prepared.
- Relax and prepare to listen to the instructions
- If you have any physical problem that may keep you from doing your best, be sure to tell the test administrator. If you are sick or in poor health, you really cannot do your best on the exam. You can come back and take the test some other time.

VII. AT THE TEST

The day of the test is here and you have the test booklet in your hand. The temptation to get going is very strong. Caution! There is more to success than knowing the right answers. You must know how to identify your papers and understand variations in the type of short-answer question used in this particular examination. Follow these suggestions for maximum results from your efforts:

1) Cooperate with the monitor

The test administrator has a duty to create a situation in which you can be as much at ease as possible. He will give instructions, tell you when to begin, check to see that you are marking your answer sheet correctly, and so on. He is not there to guard you, although he will see that your competitors do not take unfair advantage. He wants to help you do your best.

2) Listen to all instructions

Don't jump the gun! Wait until you understand all directions. In most civil service tests you get more time than you need to answer the questions. So don't be in a hurry. Read each word of instructions until you clearly understand the meaning. Study the examples, listen to all announcements and follow directions. Ask questions if you do not understand what to do.

3) Identify your papers

Civil service exams are usually identified by number only. You will be assigned a number; you must not put your name on your test papers. Be sure to copy your number correctly. Since more than one exam may be given, copy your exact examination title.

4) Plan your time

Unless you are told that a test is a "speed" or "rate of work" test, speed itself is usually not important. Time enough to answer all the questions will be provided, but this does not mean that you have all day. An overall time limit has been set. Divide the total time (in minutes) by the number of questions to determine the approximate time you have for each question.

5) Do not linger over difficult questions

If you come across a difficult question, mark it with a paper clip (useful to have along) and come back to it when you have been through the booklet. One caution if you do this – be sure to skip a number on your answer sheet as well. Check often to be sure that you have not lost your place and that you are marking in the row numbered the same as the question you are answering.

6) Read the questions

Be sure you know what the question asks! Many capable people are unsuccessful because they failed to *read* the questions correctly.

7) Answer all questions

Unless you have been instructed that a penalty will be deducted for incorrect answers, it is better to guess than to omit a question.

8) Speed tests

It is often better NOT to guess on speed tests. It has been found that on timed tests people are tempted to spend the last few seconds before time is called in marking answers at random – without even reading them – in the hope of picking up a few extra points. To discourage this practice, the instructions may warn you that your score will be "corrected" for guessing. That is, a penalty will be applied. The incorrect answers will be deducted from the correct ones, or some other penalty formula will be used.

9) Review your answers

If you finish before time is called, go back to the questions you guessed or omitted to give them further thought. Review other answers if you have time.

10) Return your test materials

If you are ready to leave before others have finished or time is called, take ALL your materials to the monitor and leave quietly. Never take any test material with you. The monitor can discover whose papers are not complete, and taking a test booklet may be grounds for disqualification.

VIII. EXAMINATION TECHNIQUES

1) Read the general instructions carefully. These are usually printed on the first page of the exam booklet. As a rule, these instructions refer to the timing of the examination; the fact that you should not start work until the signal and must stop work at a signal, etc. If there are any *special* instructions, such as a choice of questions to be answered, make sure that you note this instruction carefully.

2) When you are ready to start work on the examination, that is as soon as the signal has been given, read the instructions to each question booklet, underline any key words or phrases, such as *least, best, outline, describe* and the like. In this way you will tend to answer as requested rather than discover on reviewing your paper that you *listed without describing*, that you selected the *worst* choice rather than the *best* choice, etc.

3) If the examination is of the objective or multiple-choice type – that is, each question will also give a series of possible answers: A, B, C or D, and you are called upon to select the best answer and write the letter next to that answer on your answer paper – it is advisable to start answering each question in turn. There may be anywhere from 50 to 100 such questions in the three or four hours allotted and you can see how much time would be taken if you read through all the questions before beginning to answer any. Furthermore, if you come across a question or group of questions which you know would be difficult to answer, it would undoubtedly affect your handling of all the other questions.

4) If the examination is of the essay type and contains but a few questions, it is a moot point as to whether you should read all the questions before starting to answer any one. Of course, if you are given a choice – say five out of seven and the like – then it is essential to read all the questions so you can eliminate the two that are most difficult. If, however, you are asked to answer all the questions, there may be danger in trying to answer the easiest one first because you may find that you will spend too much time on it. The best technique is to answer the first question, then proceed to the second, etc.

5) Time your answers. Before the exam begins, write down the time it started, then add the time allowed for the examination and write down the time it must be completed, then divide the time available somewhat as follows:
   - If 3-1/2 hours are allowed, that would be 210 minutes. If you have 80 objective-type questions, that would be an average of 2-1/2 minutes per question. Allow yourself no more than 2 minutes per question, or a total of 160 minutes, which will permit about 50 minutes to review.
   - If for the time allotment of 210 minutes there are 7 essay questions to answer, that would average about 30 minutes a question. Give yourself only 25 minutes per question so that you have about 35 minutes to review.

6) The most important instruction is to *read each question* and make sure you know what is wanted. The second most important instruction is to *time yourself properly* so that you answer every question. The third most important instruction is to *answer every question*. Guess if you have to but include something for each question. Remember that you will receive no credit for a blank and will probably receive some credit if you write something in answer to an essay question. If you guess a letter – say "B" for a multiple-choice question – you may have guessed right. If you leave a blank as an answer to a multiple-choice question, the examiners may respect your feelings but it will not add a point to your score. Some exams may penalize you for wrong answers, so in such cases *only*, you may not want to guess unless you have some basis for your answer.

7) Suggestions
   a. Objective-type questions
      1. Examine the question booklet for proper sequence of pages and questions
      2. Read all instructions carefully
      3. Skip any question which seems too difficult; return to it after all other questions have been answered
      4. Apportion your time properly; do not spend too much time on any single question or group of questions

5. Note and underline key words – *all, most, fewest, least, best, worst, same, opposite,* etc.
6. Pay particular attention to negatives
7. Note unusual option, e.g., unduly long, short, complex, different or similar in content to the body of the question
8. Observe the use of "hedging" words – *probably, may, most likely,* etc.
9. Make sure that your answer is put next to the same number as the question
10. Do not second-guess unless you have good reason to believe the second answer is definitely more correct
11. Cross out original answer if you decide another answer is more accurate; do not erase until you are ready to hand your paper in
12. Answer all questions; guess unless instructed otherwise
13. Leave time for review

b. Essay questions
1. Read each question carefully
2. Determine exactly what is wanted. Underline key words or phrases.
3. Decide on outline or paragraph answer
4. Include many different points and elements unless asked to develop any one or two points or elements
5. Show impartiality by giving pros and cons unless directed to select one side only
6. Make and write down any assumptions you find necessary to answer the questions
7. Watch your English, grammar, punctuation and choice of words
8. Time your answers; don't crowd material

8) Answering the essay question

Most essay questions can be answered by framing the specific response around several key words or ideas. Here are a few such key words or ideas:

M's: manpower, materials, methods, money, management
P's: purpose, program, policy, plan, procedure, practice, problems, pitfalls, personnel, public relations

a. Six basic steps in handling problems:
1. Preliminary plan and background development
2. Collect information, data and facts
3. Analyze and interpret information, data and facts
4. Analyze and develop solutions as well as make recommendations
5. Prepare report and sell recommendations
6. Install recommendations and follow up effectiveness

b. Pitfalls to avoid
1. *Taking things for granted* – A statement of the situation does not necessarily imply that each of the elements is necessarily true; for example, a complaint may be invalid and biased so that all that can be taken for granted is that a complaint has been registered

2. *Considering only one side of a situation* – Wherever possible, indicate several alternatives and then point out the reasons you selected the best one
3. *Failing to indicate follow up* – Whenever your answer indicates action on your part, make certain that you will take proper follow-up action to see how successful your recommendations, procedures or actions turn out to be
4. *Taking too long in answering any single question* – Remember to time your answers properly

IX. AFTER THE TEST

Scoring procedures differ in detail among civil service jurisdictions although the general principles are the same. Whether the papers are hand-scored or graded by machine we have described, they are nearly always graded by number. That is, the person who marks the paper knows only the number – never the name – of the applicant. Not until all the papers have been graded will they be matched with names. If other tests, such as training and experience or oral interview ratings have been given, scores will be combined. Different parts of the examination usually have different weights. For example, the written test might count 60 percent of the final grade, and a rating of training and experience 40 percent. In many jurisdictions, veterans will have a certain number of points added to their grades.

After the final grade has been determined, the names are placed in grade order and an eligible list is established. There are various methods for resolving ties between those who get the same final grade – probably the most common is to place first the name of the person whose application was received first. Job offers are made from the eligible list in the order the names appear on it. You will be notified of your grade and your rank as soon as all these computations have been made. This will be done as rapidly as possible.

People who are found to meet the requirements in the announcement are called "eligibles." Their names are put on a list of eligible candidates. An eligible's chances of getting a job depend on how high he stands on this list and how fast agencies are filling jobs from the list.

When a job is to be filled from a list of eligibles, the agency asks for the names of people on the list of eligibles for that job. When the civil service commission receives this request, it sends to the agency the names of the three people highest on this list. Or, if the job to be filled has specialized requirements, the office sends the agency the names of the top three persons who meet these requirements from the general list.

The appointing officer makes a choice from among the three people whose names were sent to him. If the selected person accepts the appointment, the names of the others are put back on the list to be considered for future openings.

That is the rule in hiring from all kinds of eligible lists, whether they are for typist, carpenter, chemist, or something else. For every vacancy, the appointing officer has his choice of any one of the top three eligibles on the list. This explains why the person whose name is on top of the list sometimes does not get an appointment when some of the persons lower on the list do. If the appointing officer chooses the second or third eligible, the No. 1 eligible does not get a job at once, but stays on the list until he is appointed or the list is terminated.

X. HOW TO PASS THE INTERVIEW TEST

The examination for which you applied requires an oral interview test. You have already taken the written test and you are now being called for the interview test – the final part of the formal examination.

You may think that it is not possible to prepare for an interview test and that there are no procedures to follow during an interview. Our purpose is to point out some things you can do in advance that will help you and some good rules to follow and pitfalls to avoid while you are being interviewed.

What is an interview supposed to test?

The written examination is designed to test the technical knowledge and competence of the candidate; the oral is designed to evaluate intangible qualities, not readily measured otherwise, and to establish a list showing the relative fitness of each candidate – as measured against his competitors – for the position sought. Scoring is not on the basis of "right" and "wrong," but on a sliding scale of values ranging from "not passable" to "outstanding." As a matter of fact, it is possible to achieve a relatively low score without a single "incorrect" answer because of evident weakness in the qualities being measured.

Occasionally, an examination may consist entirely of an oral test – either an individual or a group oral. In such cases, information is sought concerning the technical knowledges and abilities of the candidate, since there has been no written examination for this purpose. More commonly, however, an oral test is used to supplement a written examination.

Who conducts interviews?

The composition of oral boards varies among different jurisdictions. In nearly all, a representative of the personnel department serves as chairman. One of the members of the board may be a representative of the department in which the candidate would work. In some cases, "outside experts" are used, and, frequently, a businessman or some other representative of the general public is asked to serve. Labor and management or other special groups may be represented. The aim is to secure the services of experts in the appropriate field.

However the board is composed, it is a good idea (and not at all improper or unethical) to ascertain in advance of the interview who the members are and what groups they represent. When you are introduced to them, you will have some idea of their backgrounds and interests, and at least you will not stutter and stammer over their names.

What should be done before the interview?

While knowledge about the board members is useful and takes some of the surprise element out of the interview, there is other preparation which is more substantive. It *is* possible to prepare for an oral interview – in several ways:

1) Keep a copy of your application and review it carefully before the interview

This may be the only document before the oral board, and the starting point of the interview. Know what education and experience you have listed there, and the sequence and dates of all of it. Sometimes the board will ask you to review the highlights of your experience for them; you should not have to hem and haw doing it.

2) Study the class specification and the examination announcement

Usually, the oral board has one or both of these to guide them. The qualities, characteristics or knowledges required by the position sought are stated in these documents. They offer valuable clues as to the nature of the oral interview. For example, if the job involves supervisory responsibilities, the announcement will usually indicate that knowledge of modern supervisory methods and the qualifications of the candidate as a supervisor will be tested. If so, you can expect such questions, frequently in the form of a hypothetical situation which you are expected to solve. NEVER go into an oral without knowledge of the duties and responsibilities of the job you seek.

3) **Think through each qualification required**

Try to visualize the kind of questions you would ask if you were a board member. How well could you answer them? Try especially to appraise your own knowledge and background in each area, *measured against the job sought*, and identify any areas in which you are weak. Be critical and realistic – do not flatter yourself.

4) **Do some general reading in areas in which you feel you may be weak**

For example, if the job involves supervision and your past experience has NOT, some general reading in supervisory methods and practices, particularly in the field of human relations, might be useful. Do NOT study agency procedures or detailed manuals. The oral board will be testing your understanding and capacity, not your memory.

5) **Get a good night's sleep and watch your general health and mental attitude**

You will want a clear head at the interview. Take care of a cold or any other minor ailment, and of course, no hangovers.

What should be done on the day of the interview?

Now comes the day of the interview itself. Give yourself plenty of time to get there. Plan to arrive somewhat ahead of the scheduled time, particularly if your appointment is in the fore part of the day. If a previous candidate fails to appear, the board might be ready for you a bit early. By early afternoon an oral board is almost invariably behind schedule if there are many candidates, and you may have to wait. Take along a book or magazine to read, or your application to review, but leave any extraneous material in the waiting room when you go in for your interview. In any event, relax and compose yourself.

The matter of dress is important. The board is forming impressions about you – from your experience, your manners, your attitude, and your appearance. Give your personal appearance careful attention. Dress your best, but not your flashiest. Choose conservative, appropriate clothing, and be sure it is immaculate. This is a business interview, and your appearance should indicate that you regard it as such. Besides, being well groomed and properly dressed will help boost your confidence.

Sooner or later, someone will call your name and escort you into the interview room. *This is it*. From here on you are on your own. It is too late for any more preparation. But remember, you asked for this opportunity to prove your fitness, and you are here because your request was granted.

What happens when you go in?

The usual sequence of events will be as follows: The clerk (who is often the board stenographer) will introduce you to the chairman of the oral board, who will introduce you to the other members of the board. Acknowledge the introductions before you sit down. Do not be surprised if you find a microphone facing you or a stenotypist sitting by. Oral interviews are usually recorded in the event of an appeal or other review.

Usually the chairman of the board will open the interview by reviewing the highlights of your education and work experience from your application – primarily for the benefit of the other members of the board, as well as to get the material into the record. Do not interrupt or comment unless there is an error or significant misinterpretation; if that is the case, do not hesitate. But do not quibble about insignificant matters. Also, he will usually ask you some question about your education, experience or your present job – partly to get you to start talking and to establish the interviewing "rapport." He may start the actual questioning, or turn it over to one of the other members. Frequently, each member undertakes the questioning on a particular area, one in which he is perhaps most competent, so you can expect each member to participate in the examination. Because time is limited, you may also expect some rather abrupt switches in the direction the questioning takes, so do not be upset by it. Normally, a board member will not pursue a single line of questioning unless he discovers a particular strength or weakness.

After each member has participated, the chairman will usually ask whether any member has any further questions, then will ask you if you have anything you wish to add. Unless you are expecting this question, it may floor you. Worse, it may start you off on an extended, extemporaneous speech. The board is not usually seeking more information. The question is principally to offer you a last opportunity to present further qualifications or to indicate that you have nothing to add. So, if you feel that a significant qualification or characteristic has been overlooked, it is proper to point it out in a sentence or so. Do not compliment the board on the thoroughness of their examination -- they have been sketchy, and you know it. If you wish, merely say, "No thank you, I have nothing further to add." This is a point where you can "talk yourself out" of a good impression or fail to present an important bit of information. Remember, *you close the interview yourself*.

The chairman will then say, "That is all, Mr. _____, thank you." Do not be startled; the interview is over, and quicker than you think. Thank him, gather your belongings and take your leave. Save your sigh of relief for the other side of the door.

How to put your best foot forward

Throughout this entire process, you may feel that the board individually and collectively is trying to pierce your defenses, seek out your hidden weaknesses and embarrass and confuse you. Actually, this is not true. They are obliged to make an appraisal of your qualifications for the job you are seeking, and they want to see you in your best light. Remember, they must interview all candidates and a non-cooperative candidate may become a failure in spite of their best efforts to bring out his qualifications. Here are 15 suggestions that will help you:

1) Be natural – Keep your attitude confident, not cocky

If you are not confident that you can do the job, do not expect the board to be. Do not apologize for your weaknesses, try to bring out your strong points. The board is interested in a positive, not negative, presentation. Cockiness will antagonize any board member and make him wonder if you are covering up a weakness by a false show of strength.

2) Get comfortable, but don't lounge or sprawl

Sit erectly but not stiffly. A careless posture may lead the board to conclude that you are careless in other things, or at least that you are not impressed by the importance of the occasion. Either conclusion is natural, even if incorrect. Do not fuss with your clothing, a pencil or an ashtray. Your hands may occasionally be useful to emphasize a point; do not let them become a point of distraction.

3) Do not wisecrack or make small talk

This is a serious situation, and your attitude should show that you consider it as such. Further, the time of the board is limited – they do not want to waste it, and neither should you.

4) Do not exaggerate your experience or abilities

In the first place, from information in the application or other interviews and sources, the board may know more about you than you think. Secondly, you probably will not get away with it. An experienced board is rather adept at spotting such a situation, so do not take the chance.

5) If you know a board member, do not make a point of it, yet do not hide it

Certainly you are not fooling him, and probably not the other members of the board. Do not try to take advantage of your acquaintanceship – it will probably do you little good.

6) Do not dominate the interview

Let the board do that. They will give you the clues – do not assume that you have to do all the talking. Realize that the board has a number of questions to ask you, and do not try to take up all the interview time by showing off your extensive knowledge of the answer to the first one.

7) Be attentive

You only have 20 minutes or so, and you should keep your attention at its sharpest throughout. When a member is addressing a problem or question to you, give him your undivided attention. Address your reply principally to him, but do not exclude the other board members.

8) Do not interrupt

A board member may be stating a problem for you to analyze. He will ask you a question when the time comes. Let him state the problem, and wait for the question.

9) Make sure you understand the question

Do not try to answer until you are sure what the question is. If it is not clear, restate it in your own words or ask the board member to clarify it for you. However, do not haggle about minor elements.

10) Reply promptly but not hastily

A common entry on oral board rating sheets is "candidate responded readily," or "candidate hesitated in replies." Respond as promptly and quickly as you can, but do not jump to a hasty, ill-considered answer.

11) Do not be peremptory in your answers

A brief answer is proper – but do not fire your answer back. That is a losing game from your point of view. The board member can probably ask questions much faster than you can answer them.

12) Do not try to create the answer you think the board member wants

He is interested in what kind of mind you have and how it works – not in playing games. Furthermore, he can usually spot this practice and will actually grade you down on it.

13) Do not switch sides in your reply merely to agree with a board member

Frequently, a member will take a contrary position merely to draw you out and to see if you are willing and able to defend your point of view. Do not start a debate, yet do not surrender a good position. If a position is worth taking, it is worth defending.

14) Do not be afraid to admit an error in judgment if you are shown to be wrong

The board knows that you are forced to reply without any opportunity for careful consideration. Your answer may be demonstrably wrong. If so, admit it and get on with the interview.

15) Do not dwell at length on your present job

The opening question may relate to your present assignment. Answer the question but do not go into an extended discussion. You are being examined for a *new* job, not your present one. As a matter of fact, try to phrase ALL your answers in terms of the job for which you are being examined.

Basis of Rating

Probably you will forget most of these "do's" and "don'ts" when you walk into the oral interview room. Even remembering them all will not ensure you a passing grade. Perhaps you did not have the qualifications in the first place. But remembering them will help you to put your best foot forward, without treading on the toes of the board members.

Rumor and popular opinion to the contrary notwithstanding, an oral board wants you to make the best appearance possible. They know you are under pressure – but they also want to see how you respond to it as a guide to what your reaction would be under the pressures of the job you seek. They will be influenced by the degree of poise you display, the personal traits you show and the manner in which you respond.

ABOUT THIS BOOK

This book contains tests divided into Examination Sections. Go through each test, answering every question in the margin. We have also attached a sample answer sheet at the back of the book that can be removed and used. At the end of each test look at the answer key and check your answers. On the ones you got wrong, look at the right answer choice and learn. Do not fill in the answers first. Do not memorize the questions and answers, but understand the answer and principles involved. On your test, the questions will likely be different from the samples. Questions are changed and new ones added. If you understand these past questions you should have success with any changes that arise. Tests may consist of several types of questions. We have additional books on each subject should more study be advisable or necessary for you. Finally, the more you study, the better prepared you will be. This book is intended to be the last thing you study before you walk into the examination room. Prior study of relevant texts is also recommended. NLC publishes some of these in our Fundamental Series. Knowledge and good sense are important factors in passing your exam. Good luck also helps. So now study this Passbook, absorb the material contained within and take that knowledge into the examination. Then do your best to pass that exam.

EXAMINATION SECTION

EXAMINATION SECTION
TEST 1

DIRECTIONS: Each question or incomplete statement is followed by several suggested answers or completions. Select the one that BEST answers the question or completes the statement. *PRINT THE LETTER OF THE CORRECT ANSWER IN THE SPACE AT THE RIGHT.*

1. You have recently been assigned to a new office and are expected to supervise six clerks.
   All of the following would be good introductory steps to take EXCEPT

   A. giving a clear presentation of yourself to the clerks, including a short summary of your recent work experience
   B. initiating informal discussions with each clerk concerning his work
   C. making a general survey of all the functions which each clerk has been performing
   D. making a list of the duties each clerk is required to perform and giving it to the clerk

   1.____

2. Your supervisor has advised you that a specific aspect of a job is being done incorrectly and you acknowledge the mistake.
   Of the following, the MOST efficient way of dealing with this situation is to

   A. call a meeting of the clerks who are performing this particular function and explain the correct method
   B. assume the blame and correct the errors as they are given to you
   C. speak with each clerk individually and carefully show each one the proper method
   D. distribute a set of written instructions covering all clerical procedures to the employees doing that particular job

   2.____

3. A new department regulation calls for a change in a particular method of processing new applications. Two clerks have complained to you that the new method is more time-consuming, and they prefer to do it the original way.
   Of the following, what is the MOST advisable thing to do?

   A. Discuss the situation with them and attempt to determine whether they are utilizing the method properly.
   B. Discuss the advantages of both methods with them and let them use the one that is more practical.
   C. Firmly instruct the clerks to proceed with the new method since it is not up to them to refute department policy.
   D. Tell them to survey the opinions of the other clerks on this matter and inform you of the results.

   3.____

4. A member of the clerical staff has recently begun reporting late for work rather regularly. On each occasion, the individual presented an excuse, but the latenesses continue.
   Of the following, the MOST advisable action for her supervisor to take is to

   A. have a staff meeting and stress the importance of being on time for work, without singling out the specific individual
   B. put a notice on the departmental office bulletin board, specifying and stressing that lateness can not be tolerated

   4.____

1

C. talk privately with the individual to determine whether there are any unusual circumstances that might be causing the lateness
D. send the individual a memorandum clearly indicating that continual lateness will result in disciplinary action

5. Assume that, as the supervisor of a unit, you have been asked to prepare a vacation schedule for your subordinate employees. The employees have had different lengths of service. Some of them have already submitted requests for certain weeks.
Of the following, which factor would be LEAST important in setting up this schedule?

    A. Your opinion of each employee's past work performance
    B. Each employee's preference for a vacation period
    C. The amount of work the unit is expected to accomplish during the vacation period
    D. The number of employees who have requested to go on vacation at the same time

6. Your superior finds that he must leave the office one day before he has had time to check and sign the day's correspondence. He asks you to proofread the letters, have corrections made where necessary, and then sign his name. You have never signed his name before.
Of the following, the BEST thing for you to do is to

    A. sign your superior's name in full, making it look as much like his handwriting as possible
    B. sign your superior's name and your own name in full as proof that you signed for him
    C. sign your superior's name in full and add your initials to show that the signature is not his own
    D. politely refuse to sign his name because it is forgery

7. The head of your office sometimes makes handwritten notations on original letters which he receives and requests that you mail the letters back to the sender. Of the following, the BEST action for you to take FIRST is to

    A. request that this practice be stopped because it does not provide for a record in the files
    B. request that this practice be stopped because it is not the customary way to respond to letters
    C. photocopy the letters so that there are copies for the file and then send the letters out
    D. ask the head of your office if he wants you to keep any record of the letters

8. The main function of most agency administrative offices is *information management.* Information that is received by an administrative office may be classified as active (information which requires the recipient to take some action) or passive (information which does not require action).
Which one of the following items received must clearly be treated as ACTIVE information?
A(n)

    A. confirmation of payment
    B. press release concerning an agency event
    C. advertisement for a new restaurant opening near the agency
    D. request for a student transcript

9. Which of the following statements about the use of the photocopy process is COR- 9.____
   RECT?

   A. It is difficult to use.
   B. It can be used to reproduce color.
   C. It does not print well on colored paper.
   D. Once source documents have been used, they cannot be used again.

10. In order to get the BEST estimate of how long a repetitive office procedure should take, a 10.____
    supervisor should find out how

    A. long it takes her best worker to do the procedure once on a typical day
    B. long it takes her best and worst workers to do the procedure once on a typical day
    C. much time her best worker spends on the procedure during a typical week and the total number of times the worker executes the procedure during the same week
    D. much time all her subordinates spend on the procedure during a typical week and the total number of times the procedure was executed during the same week by all employees

11. Of the following, the MOST suitable and appropriate way to make 250 copies of a partic- 11.____
    ular form is to

    A. print all 250 copies on the office computer
    B. delegate the work to someone else
    C. reproduce it on a photocopying machine
    D. use an offset printing process

Questions 12-18.

DIRECTIONS: Questions 12 through 18 are to be answered on the basis of the extracts shown below from Federal withholding tables. These tables indicate the amounts which must be withheld from the employee's salary by his employer for Federal income tax and for social security. They are based on weekly earnings.

INCOME TAX WITHHOLDING TABLE

The wages are -		And the number of withholding exemptions claimed is-					
At least	But less than	0	1	2	3	4	5
		The amount of income tax to be withheld shall be -					
$200	$205	$14.10	$11.80	$ 9.50	$ 7.20	$ 4.90	$2.80
205	210	14.90	12.60	10.30	8.00	5.70	3.50
210	215	15.70	13.40	11.10	8.80	6.50	4.20
215	220	16.50	14.20	11.90	9.60	7.30	5.00
220	225	17.30	15.00	12.70	10.40	8.10	5.80
225	230	18.10	15.80	13.50	11.20	8.90	6.60
230	235	18.90	16.60	14.30	12.00	9.70	7.40
235	240	19.70	17.40	15.10	12.80	10.50	8.20
240	245	20.50	18.20	15.90	13.60	11.30	9.00
245	250	21.30	19.00	16.70	14.40	12.10	9.80

SOCIAL SECURITY EMPLOYEE TAX TABLE

Wages		Tax to be withheld	Wages		Tax to be withheld
At least	But less than		At least	But less than	
$202.79	$202.99	$15.35	$229.72	$229.91	$16.75
202.99	203.18	15.36	229.91	230.10	16.76
203.18	203.37	15.37	230.10	230.29	16.77
203.37	203.56	15.38	230.29	230.49	16.78
203.56	203.75	15.39	230.49	230.68	16.79
203.75	203.95	15.40	230.68	230.87	16.80
203.95	204.14	15.41	230.87	231.06	16.81
204.14	204.33	15.42	231.06	231.25	16.82
204.33	204.52	15.43	231.25	231.45	16.83
204.52	204.72	15.44	231.45	231.64	16.84

Wages		Tax to be withheld	Wages		Tax to be withheld
At least	But less than		At least	But less than	
$222.02	$222.22	$16.35	$234.52	$234.72	$17.00
222.22	222.41	16.36	234.72	234.91	17.01
222.41	222.60	16.37	234.91	235.10	17.02
222.60	222.79	16.38	235.10	235.29	17.03
222.79	222.99	16.39	235.29	235.49	17.04
222.99	223.18	16.40	235.49	235.68	17.05
223.18	223.37	16.41	235.68	235.87	17.06
223.37	223.56	16.42	235.87	236.06	17.07
223.56	223.75	16.43	236.06	236.25	17.08
223.75	223.95	16.44	236.25	236.45	17.09

12. Dave Andes has wages of $242.75 for one week. He has claimed three withholding exemptions.
What is the Federal income tax which should be withheld?

   A. $13.60   B. $15.90   C. $18.20   D. $20.50

12._____

13. Mary Hodes has wages of $229.95 for one week.
What is the Social Security tax which should be withheld?

   A. $16.75   B. $16.76   C. $16.77   D. $16.78

13._____

14. Joe Jones had wages of $235.63 for one week. He has claimed two withholding exemptions.
What is the Federal income tax which should be withheld?

   A. $12.80   B. $14.30   C. $15.10   D. $17.40

14._____

15. Tom Stein had wages of $203.95 for one week. What is the Social Security tax which should be withheld?

   A. $15.40   B. $15.41   C. $16.05   D. $16.06

15._____

16. Robert Helman had wages of $222.80 for one week. He has claimed one withholding exemption.
If only Federal income tax and Social Security tax were deducted from his earnings for the same week, how much *take-home* pay should he have for the week?

   A. $191.41   B. $193.96   C. $194.12   D. $195.65

16._____

17. Audrey Stein has wages of $203.00 for one week. She claimed no withholding exemptions.
If only Federal income tax and Social Security tax were deducted from her earnings for the same week, how much *take-home* pay should she have for the week?

   A. $171.84   B. $172.34   C. $173.54   D. $175.84

17._____

18. Anthony Covallo, who worked 28 hours in the past week, has a regular hourly rate of $7.25 per hour and earns a premium of time and a half for hours over 40. He has claimed four withholding exemptions.
After Social Security tax and Federal income tax are deducted from his wages for the past week, how much pay does he have left?

   A. $180.98   B. $181.13   C. $182.29   D. $182.74

18._____

19. In judging the adequacy of a standard office form, which of the following is LEAST important?
_____ of the form.

   A. Date   B. Legibility   C. Size   D. Design

19._____

20. Clear and accurate telephone messages should be taken for employees who are out of the office.
Which of the following is of LEAST importance when taking a telephone message?

   A. Name of the person called
   B. Name of the caller

20._____

5

C. Details of the message
D. Time of the call

21. Suppose that all office supplies are kept in a centrally located cabinet in the office. Of the following, which is usually the BEST policy to adhere to for distribution of supplies?

    A. Permit employees to stock up on all supplies to avoid frequent trips to the cabinet.
    B. Assign one employee to be in charge of distributing all supplies to other employees at frequent intervals.
    C. Inform employees that supplies should be taken in large quantities and only when needed.
    D. Keep cabinet closed and instruct employees that they must check with you before taking supplies.

Questions 22-25.

DIRECTIONS: Questions 22 through 25 are to be answered SOLELY on the basis of the following passage.

Use of the systems and procedures approach to office management is revolutionizing the supervision of office work. This approach views an enterprise as an entity which seeks to fulfill definite objectives. Systems and procedures help to organize repetitive work into a routine, thus reducing the amount of decision-making required for its accomplishment. As a result, employees are guided in their efforts and perform only necessary work. Supervisors are relieved of any details of execution and are free to attend to more important work. Establishing work guides which require that identical tasks be performed the same way each, time permits standardization of forms, machine operations, work methods, and controls. This approach also reduces the probability of errors. Any error committed is usually discovered quickly because the incorrect work does not meet the requirement of the work guides. Errors are also reduced through work specialization which allows each employee to become thoroughly proficient in a particular type of work. Such proficiency also tends to improve the morale of the employees.

22. Of the following, which one BEST expresses the main theme of the above passage? The

    A. advantages and disadvantages of the systems and procedures approach to office management
    B. effectiveness of the systems and procedures approach to office management in developing skills
    C. systems and procedures approach to office management as it relates to office costs
    D. advantages of the systems and procedures approach to office management for supervisors and office workers

23. Work guides are LEAST likely to be used when

    A. standardized forms are used
    B. a particular office task is distinct and different from all others
    C. identical tasks are to be performed in identical ways
    D. similar work methods are expected from each employee

24. According to the above passage, when an employee makes a work error, it USUALLY   24.____

    A. is quickly corrected by the supervisor
    B. necessitates a change in the work guides
    C. can be detected quickly if work guides are in use
    D. increases the probability of further errors by that employee

25. The above passage states that the accuracy of an employee's work is INCREASED by   25.____

    A. using the work specialization approach
    B. employing a probability sample
    C. requiring him to shift at one time into different types of tasks
    D. having his supervisor check each detail of work execution

---

KEY (CORRECT ANSWERS)

1.	D	11.	C
2.	A	12.	A
3.	A	13.	B
4.	C	14.	C
5.	A	15.	B
6.	C	16.	A
7.	D	17.	C
8.	D	18.	D
9.	B	19.	A
10.	D	20.	D

21. B
22. D
23. B
24. C
25. A

TEST 2

DIRECTIONS: Each question or incomplete statement is followed by several suggested answers or completions. Select the one that BEST answers the question or completes the statement. *PRINT THE LETTER OF THE CORRECT ANSWER IN THE SPACE AT THE RIGHT.*

1. A certain supervisor often holds group meetings with subordinates to discuss the goals of the unit and manpower requirements for meeting objectives.
   For the supervisor to hold such meetings is a

   A. *good* practice because it will aid both the supervisor and subordinates in planning and completing the unit's work
   B. *good* practice because it will prevent future problems from interfering with the unit's objectives
   C. *poor* practice because the supervisor has the sole responsibility for meeting objectives and should make manpower decisions without any advice
   D. *poor* practice because the subordinates will be allowed to set their own work quotas

   1.____

2. Assume that you are a supervisor who has been asked to evaluate the work of a clerk who was transferred to your unit about six months ago.
   Which one of the following, by itself, provides the BEST basis for making such an evaluation?

   A. Ask the clerk's former supervisor about the employee's previous work.
   B. Ask the clerk's co-workers for their opinions of the employee's work.
   C. Evaluate the quantity and quality of the employee's work over the six-month period.
   D. Observe the employee's performance from time to time during the next week and base your evaluation on these observations.

   2.____

3. Which of the following would be the MOST desirable way for a supervisor to help improve the job performance of a particular subordinate?

   A. Criticize the employee's performance in front of other employees.
   B. Privately warn the employee that failure to meet work standards may lead to dismissal.
   C. Hold a meeting with this employee and other subordinates in which the need to improve the unit's performance is stressed.
   D. Meet privately with the employee and discuss both positive and negative aspects of the employee's work

   3.____

4. Suppose that your office has a limited supply of a pamphlet which people may read in your office when they seek certain information, but another office in your building is supposed to have a large supply available for distribution to the public.
   Which of the following would be the BEST thing for you to do when someone states that he has not been able to obtain one of these pamphlets?

   A. Tell him that he misunderstood the directions that other employees have given him and carefully direct him to the other office.
   B. Ask whether he has visited the other office and requested a copy from them.
   C. Let him take one of your office's copies of the pamphlet and then call the other office and ask why they have run out of copies for distribution.

   4.____

D. Tell him that your office does its best to keep the public informed but that this might not be true of other offices.

5. On Monday, a clerk made many errors in completing a new daily record form. The supervisor explained the errors and had the clerk correct the form. On Tuesday, the clerk made fewer errors. Because he was very busy, the supervisor did not point out the errors to the clerk but corrected the errors himself. On Wednesday, the clerk made the same number of errors as on Tuesday. The supervisor reprimanded the clerk for making so many errors.
The supervisor's handling of this situation on Wednesday may be considered poor MAINLY because the

   A. clerk was not given enough time to complete each form properly
   B. supervisor should not have expected improvement without further training
   C. clerk was obviously incapable of completing the form
   D. supervisor should have continued to correct the errors himself

Questions 6-8.

DIRECTIONS: Questions 6 through 8 are to be answered SOLELY on the basis of the information contained in the following passage.

When using words like company, association, council, committee, and board in place of the full official name, the writer should not capitalize these short forms unless he intends them to invoke the full force of the institution's authority. In legal contracts, in minutes, or in formal correspondence where one is speaking formally and officially on behalf of the company, the term "Company" is usually capitalized, but in ordinary usage, where it is not essential to load the short form with this significance, capitalization would be excessive. (Example: The company will have many good openings for graduates this June.)

The treatment recommended for short forms of place names is essentially the same as that recommended for short forms of organizational names. In general, we capitalize the full form but not the short form. If Park Avenue is referred to in one sentence, then "the avenue" is sufficient in subsequent references. The same is true with words like building, hotel, station, and airport, which are capitalized when part of a proper name (Pan Am Building, Hotel Plaza, Union Station, O'Hare Airport) but are simply lower-cased when replacing these specific names.

6. The above passage states that USUALLY the short forms of names of organizations

   A. and places should not be capitalized
   B. and places should be capitalized
   C. should not be capitalized, but the short forms of names of places should be capitalized
   D. should be capitalized, but the short forms of names of places should not be capitalized

7. The above passage states that in legal contracts, in minutes, and in formal correspondence, the short forms of names of organizations should

   A. usually not be capitalized
   B. usually be capitalized
   C. usually not be used
   D. never be used

8. It can be INFERRED from the above passage that decisions regarding when to capitalize certain words

   A. should be left to the discretion of the writer
   B. should be based on generally accepted rules
   C. depend on the total number of words capitalized
   D. are of minor importance

9. The Central Terminal and the Gardens Terminal are located on Glover Street.
   In ordinary usage, if this sentence were to be followed by the sentence in the choices below, which form of the sentence would be CORRECT?

   A. Both Terminals are situated on the same street.
   B. Both terminals are situated on the same Street.
   C. Both terminals are situated on the same street.
   D. Both Terminals are situated on the same Street.

10. A stylus is a(n)

    A. implement for writing containing a cylinder of graphite
    B. implement for writing with ink or a similar fluid
    C. pointed implement used to write
    D. stick of colored wax used for writing

11. As a supervisor, you have the responsibility of teaching new employees the functions and procedures of your office after their orientation by the personnel office.
    Of the following, the BEST way to begin such instruction is to

    A. advise the new employee of the benefits and services available to him, over and above his salary
    B. discuss the negative aspects of the departmental procedures and indicate methods available to overcome them
    C. assist the new employee in understanding the general purpose of the office procedures and how they fit in with the overall operation
    D. give a detailed briefing of the operations of your office, its functions and procedures

12. Assume that you are the supervisor of a clerical unit. One of the duties of the employees in your unit is to conduct a brief interview with persons using the services of your agency for the first time. The purpose of the interview is to get general background information in order to best direct them to the appropriate division.
    A clerk comes to your office and says that a prospective client has just called her some rather unpleasant names, accused her of being nosey and meddlesome, and has stated emphatically that she refuses to talk with an *underling,* meaning the clerk. The young woman is almost in tears. Of the following, what is the FIRST action you should take?

    A. Immediately call the agency's protection officer, have him advise the client of the regulations, and tell her that she will be removed if she is not more polite.
    B. Calm the clerk, introduce yourself to the client, and quietly discuss the agency's services, regulations, and informational needs, and request that she complete the interview with the clerk.

C. Calm the clerk, have her return and firmly advise the client of the agency's rules concerning the need for this first interview.
D. Introduce yourself to the client and advise her that without an apology to the clerk and completion of the interview, she will not be given any service.

13. A recent high school graduate has just been assigned to the unit which you supervise. Which of the following would be the LEAST desirable technique to use with this employee?   13.____

    A. At any one time, give the new employee only as much detail about the job as the employee can absorb.
    B. Always tell the new employee the correct procedure, then demonstrate how it is accomplished.
    C. Assign the employee the same quantity and type of work that the other employees are doing to see if the employee can handle the job.
    D. Assume the employee is tense and be prepared to repeat procedures and descriptions.

14. Assume that you supervise a work unit of several employees. Which of the following is LEAST essential in assuring that the goals which you set for the unit are achieved?   14.____

    A. Establishing objectives and standards for the staff
    B. Providing justification for disciplinary action
    C. Measuring performance or progress of individuals against standards
    D. Taking corrective action where performance is less than expected

15. One of the clerks you supervise is often reluctant to accept assignments and usually complains about the amount of work expected, although the other clerks with the same assignments and workload seem quite happy.   15.____
    Of the following, the MOST accurate assumption that you can make about this clerk is that she

    A. will require additional observation and help
    B. will eventually have to be discharged or transferred
    C. is incompetent
    D. is overworked

Questions 16-21.

DIRECTIONS: Questions 16 through 21 are to be answered SOLELY on the basis of the airline timetable and the information appearing on the last page of this test.

Fact Situation:
An administrator wants you to purchase airline tickets for him so that he can attend a meeting being held in Chicago on Monday. He must leave from LaGuardia Airport in New York on Monday morning as late as possible but with arrival in Chicago no later than 9:00 A.M. He wishes to fly coach/economy class both ways. The meeting is due to end at 5:30 P.M., and he wishes to obtain the first plane after 6:45 P.M. going back to LaGuardia Airport. If all these requirements have been met, he would, if possible, also like to fly to and leave from Midway Airport in Chicago and go non-stop both ways.

16. You should obtain a ticket for the administrator from New York to Chicago on flight number

    A. 483   B. 201   C. 277   D. 539

17. You should obtain a ticket for the administrator from Chicago to New York on flight number

    A. 588   B. 692   C. 268   D. 334

18. The administrator decides to take limousines to and from both airports.
    If the limousine charge in Chicago is $52.50. and there is no reduced rate for a round-trip flight, what is the cost of the administrator's round-trip air fare PLUS limousine service?

    A. $827.50   B. $931.00   C. $963.00   D. $967.00

19. The administrator asked you whether he would be able to get breakfast on his flight to Chicago or whether he should go to the airport early and eat there before boarding the plane. He prefers to eat on the plane.
    Of the following, the BEST reply to make is:

    A. I will have to telephone the airport to find out
    B. You should eat at the airport
    C. A meal is served on the plane
    D. Only certain passengers get a meal on the plane

20. Of the following requests of the administrator concerning his travel arrangements, which one is IMPOSSIBLE to meet?

    A. Chicago arrival no later than 9 A.M.
    B. New York departure from LaGuardia Airport
    C. Non-stop flights both ways
    D. Chicago departure from Midway Airport

21. Suppose that it is necessary to take a first-class seat on the trip to Chicago although you have no problem reserving a coach/economy seat on the return trip.
    If there is no reduction in fare for round-trip flights, how much MORE will this trip cost than round-trip coach/ economy?

    A. $209   B. $236   C. $318   D. $636

22. Ms. X, a clerk under your supervision, has been working in the unit for a few weeks. Some of the other employees have complained to you that Ms. X has an annoying habit of constantly tapping her feet on the floor and it disturbs their work.
    The BEST thing for you to do is to

    A. ignore the complaints because the employees should be concerned only with their own habits
    B. speak with Ms. X privately and discuss the situation with her
    C. make a general announcement that employees should control their nervous habits
    D. observe Ms. X for a few weeks to see if the employees are correct, and then take action

23. Suppose you answer a telephone call from someone who states that he is a friend of one of your co-workers and needs the employee's new address in order to send an invitation. Your co-worker is on vacation but you know her address.
    Which of the following is the BEST action for you to take?

    A. Give the caller the address but ask the caller not to mention that you are the one who gave it out.
    B. Give the caller the address and leave a note for your co-worker stating what you did.
    C. Tell the caller you do not know the address but will give the employee's phone number if that will help.
    D. Offer to take his name and address and have your co-worker contact him.

24. Assume that you receive a telephone call in which the caller requests information which you know is posted in the office next to yours. You start to tell the caller you will transfer her call to the right office, but she interrupts you and says she has been transferred from office to office and is tired of getting a *run-around*. Of the following, the BEST thing for you to do is to

    A. give the caller the phone number of the office next to yours and quickly end the conversation
    B. give her the phone number of the office next to yours and tell her you will try to transfer her call
    C. ask her if she wants to hold on while you get the information for her
    D. tell the caller that she could have avoided the *run-around* by asking for the right office, and suggest that she come in person

25. Assume that your unit processes confidential forms which are submitted by persons seeking financial assistance. An individual comes to your office, gives you his name, and states that he would like to look over a form which he sent in about a week ago because he believes he omitted some important information.
    Of the following, the BEST thing for you to do FIRST is to

    A. locate the proper form
    B. call the individual's home telephone number to verify his identity
    C. ask the individual if he has proof of his identity
    D. call the security office

KEY (CORRECT ANSWERS)

1.	A		11.	C
2.	C		12.	B
3.	D		13.	C
4.	B		14.	B
5.	B		15.	A
6.	A		16.	A
7.	B		17.	D
8.	B		18.	B
9.	C		19.	C
10.	C		20.	D

21.	C
22.	B
23.	D
24.	C
25.	C

EXAMINATION SECTION

TEST 1

DIRECTIONS: Each question or incomplete statement is followed by several suggested answers or completions. Select the one that BEST answers the question or completes the statement. *PRINT THE LETTER OF THE CORRECT ANSWER IN THE SPACE AT THE RIGHT.*

Questions 1-20.

DIRECTIONS: Listed below in T accounts are the five MAJOR classifications of accounts. Consider carefully each of the following statements and indicate the change by writing the appropriate letter from the T accounts in the space at the right.

ASSETS	LIABILITIES	PROPRIETORSHIP	INCOME	EXPENSES
A | B	C | D	E | F	G | H	I | J

Sample Question:
A decrease in cash
The CORRECT answer is B.

1. An increase in equipment   1.____

2. An increase in the proprietorship   2.____

3. An increase in office salaries   3.____

4. A decrease in accounts payable   4.____

5. An increase in merchandise inventory   5.____

6. A decrease in office equipment   6.____

7. A decrease in office supplies   7.____

8. An increase in the proprietor's drawing account   8.____

9. A withdrawal of capital by the proprietor   9.____

10. An increase in sales   10.____

11. An increase in salaries payable   11.____

12. An increase in the net profit for the period   12.____

13. An increase in the sales returns and allowances   13.____

2 (#1)

14. A decrease in purchases   14.____

15. A decrease in the accounts receivable   15.____

16. An increase in the mortgage payable   16.____

17. An increase in delivery expense   17.____

18. An increase in notes payable   18.____

19. An increase in purchases returns and allowances   19.____

20. A decrease in delivery equipment   20.____

Questions 21-40.

DIRECTIONS: Indicate the title of the accounts to be debited and credited in journalizing, adjusting, and closing the transactions given below by writing in the space at the right the letters that correspond to the accounts listed at the right.

Sample Question:
Paid the rent for the month, $100   Debit   Credit
                                           K   C

			Debit	Credit
21.	C.M. Smith invested $10,000 in the business	A. Accounts Payable	21.____	____
		B. Accounts Receivable		
		C. Cash		
22.	Purchased merchandise on account from A.D. Hall, $875	D. Income & Expense Summary	22.____	____
		E. Insurance		
23.	Sold merchandise on account to L.S. Brook, $500	F. Insurance Expense	23.____	____
		G. Merchandise Inventory		
24.	Received $250 from cash sales	H. Office Supplies	24.____	____
		I. Office Supplies Used		
25.	Purchased office supplies for cash, $90	J. Purchases	25.____	____
		K. Rent Expense		
26.	Paid A.D. Hall $500 to apply on account	L. Salaries	26.____	____
		M. Salaries Payable		
		N. Sales		
27.	Paid insurance premium for the year, $360	O. C.M. Smith, Capital	27.____	____
		P. C.M. Smith, Drawing		
28.	Paid C.M. Smith $100 for personal use		28.____	____
29.	Received $300 from L.S. Brooks, to apply on account		29.____	____

3 (#1)

30. Paid salaries for the month $500   30. ____ ____

Adjusting Entries

31. The supplies used during the month   31. ____ ____
    were $60

32. The salaries owed at the close of   32. ____ ____
    the month were $40

33. The prepaid insurance expired was $30   33. ____ ____

34. The beginning merchandise inventory   34. ____ ____
    was $1200

35. The closing merchandise inventory   35. ____ ____
    was $750

Closing Entries

36. The sales account has a balance   36. ____ ____
    of $4500

37. The salaries for the month were $540   37. ____ ____

38. The purchase account balance is $3600   38. ____ ____

39. The office supplies used were $75   39. ____ ____

40. The income and expense summary has   40. ____ ____
    a net profit of $350

KEY (CORRECT ANSWERS)

					DEBIT	CREDIT		DEBIT	CREDIT
1.	A	11.	D	21.	C	O	31.	I	H
2.	F	12.	F	22.	J	A	32.	L	M
3.	I	13.	G	23.	B	N	33.	F	E
4.	C	14.	J	24.	C	N	34.	D	G
5.	A	15.	B	25.	H	C	35.	G	D
6.	B	16.	D	26.	A	C	36.	N	D
7.	B	17.	I	27.	E	C	37.	D	L
8.	E	18.	D	28.	P	C	38.	D	J
9.	E	19.	J	29.	C	B	39.	D	I
10.	H	20.	B	30.	L	C	40.	D	O

TEST 2

DIRECTIONS: Each question or incomplete statement is followed by several suggested answers or completions. Select the one that BEST answers the question or completes the statement. *PRINT THE LETTER OF THE CORRECT ANSWER IN THE SPACE AT THE RIGHT.*

Questions 1-16.

DIRECTIONS: Read each statement carefully. If you believe that the account should be debited, place a D for DEBIT in the space at the right. If you think it should be credited, place a C for CREDIT in the space at the right.

1. When sales are made for cash, the sales account is (debited or credited). 1.____

2. When sales are made on account, the customer's account is (debited or credited). 2.____

3. When merchandise is purchased for cash, the purchases account is (debited or credited). 3.____

4. The creditor's account is (debited or credited) when payment is made on account. 4.____

5. The sales account is (debited or credited) for the total of the amount column in the Sales Journal. 5.____

6. The cash account is (debited or credited) for the total of the cash column in the Cash Receipts Journal. 6.____

7. The purchases account is (debited or credited) for the total amount of the purchases column in the Purchases Journal. 7.____

8. The accounts receivable account is (debited or credited) for the total amount of the Sales Journal. 8.____

9. Each account in the Sales Journal is posted to the (debit or credit) of the customer's account. 9.____

10. The total of the accounts payable column in the Cash Payments Journal is posted to the (debit or credit) of the accounts payable account. 10.____

11. The total of the cash column in the Cash Payments Journal is posted to the (debit or credit) of the cash account. 11.____

12. Each account with an amount entered in the General column of the Cash Receipts Journal is (debited or credited). 12.____

2 (#2)

13. When the proprietor invests additional cash in the business, the capital account is (debited or credited).   13.____

14. When merchandise is purchased on account, the purchases account is (debited or credited).   14.____

15. When sales salaries are unpaid at the close of the fiscal period, the salaries payable account is (debited or credited).   15.____

16. When equipment is purchased on account, the creditor's account is (debited or credited).   16.____

Questions 17-30.

DIRECTIONS: The following figures have been taken from Income Statements. Certain figures have been omitted and letters have been substituted. Determine the CORRECT amounts that should be recorded for each of the letters and write this amount in the space at the right. Each line across the page is a separate income statement.

Sales	Beginning Inventory	Purchases	Closing Inventory	Cost of Goods Sold	Gross Profit	Expenses	Net Profit	Net Loss
22,000	8,000	12,000	A	15,000	B	4,000	C	
D	E	60,000	30,000	40,000	10,000	F		2,000
3,500	1,000	2,500	500	G	500	H	100	
7,500	500	I	2,000	J	1,000	800	K	
30,000	L	25,000	5,000	28,000	M	2,500		N

17. A   17.____

18. B   18.____

19. C   19.____

20. D   20.____

21. E   21.____

22. F   22.____

23. G   23.____

24. H   24.____

25. I   25.____

26. J   26.____

27. K   27.____
28. L   28.____
29. M   29.____
30. N   30.____

KEY (CORRECT ANSWERS)

1.	C	11.	C	21.	10,000
2.	D	12.	C	22.	12,000
3.	D	13.	C	23.	3,000
4.	D	14.	D	24.	400
5.	C	15.	C	25.	8,000
6.	D	16.	C	26.	6,500
7.	D	17.	5,000	27.	200
8.	D	18.	7,000	28.	8,000
9.	D	19.	3,000	29.	2,000
10.	D	20.	50,000	30.	500

TEST 3

Questions 1-25

DIRECTIONS: Each of Questions 1 through 25 consists of a statement. You are to indicate whether the statement is TRUE (T) or FALSE (F). *PRINT THE LETTER OF THE CORRECT ANSWER IN THE SPACE AT THE RIGHT.*

1. One of the primary objectives of the proprietor of a business is to increase his proprietorship by earning a profit.   1.____

2. The length of time covered by the Income and Expense Statement is of no importance or significance.   2.____

3. The length of time covered by the Balance Sheet is of no importance or significance.   3.____

4. When a customer takes advantage of a cash discount, the amount of cash received is more than the amount of the invoice for which payment is received.   4.____

5. Posting of column totals from the Cash Receipts Journal to the General Ledger is done each day.   5.____

6. After the adjustments have been entered in their appropriate column in the worksheet, their equality is proved by adding the columns.   6.____

7. The amount of unsold merchandise is found by subtracting the merchandise sales from the merchandise purchased.   7.____

8. In the Income and Expense Statement, the sales minus the cost of goods sold equals the gross profit.   8.____

9. If the operating expenses exceed the gross profit, a net loss results.   9.____

10. Only asset, liability, and capital accounts appear in the post-closing trial balance.   10.____

11. The earning of a net profit by a business results in an increase in the net worth of the business.   11.____

12. If the assets of a business are less than the liabilities, the business is solvent.   12.____

13. Small business can use accounting and data processing machines to a better advantage than large businesses.   13.____

14. The adjusting entries can be prepared from the adjustment columns of the worksheet.   14.____

15. The amount of the supplies used during the fiscal period is credited to the supplies account at the close of the fiscal period.   15.____

16. If the credit side of the income and expense summary account is larger than the debit side, the difference is a net loss to the business.   16.____

17. The discount on sales is considered to be a part of the regular operating expenses of the business.   17.____

18. In writing off a customer's uncollectible amount, the allowance for bad debts in the General Ledger is credited.   18.____

19. The amount credited to the allowance for bad debts account is an estimated amount.   19.____

20. The allowance for depreciation account usually has a credit balance.   20.____

21. The time received for a fixed asset at the time it is replaced is always equal to its book value.   21.____

22. Prepaid expenses are sometimes called deferred credits to income.   22.____

23. Expenses that are incurred but not paid are termed accrued expenses.   23.____

24. Prepaid expenses may be shown on the balance sheet as a current asset.   24.____

25. Equipment is listed on the balance sheet as a fixed asset.   25.____

Questions 26-30.

DIRECTIONS: Questions 26 through 30 are to be answered by writing the CORRECT amount in the space at the right.

26. The office supplies account has a balance of $150 at the close of the fiscal period. The actual inventory of supplies is $60. What is the amount of supplies used during the period?   26.____

27. A company receives $490 in cash from a customer for the prompt payment of an invoice. Two percent was the discount. What was the original amount of the invoice?   27.____

28. The balance of the store supplies before adjustment is $400. The total cost of the store supplies on hand at the end of the period is $150. What is the amount of the adjusting entry?   28.____

29. What is the amount necessary to pay a $300 invoice, terms 3/10, 2/20, n/30, twelve days after date?

29._____

30. If equipment costing $1,500, with an estimated life of ten years, was purchased, what is the annual rate of depreciation?

30._____

KEY (CORRECT ANSWERS)

1.	T	11.	T	21.	F
2.	F	12.	F	22.	F
3.	T	13.	F	23.	T
4.	F	14.	T	24.	T
5.	F	15.	T	25.	T
6.	T	16.	F	26.	$90
7.	F	17.	F	27.	$500
8.	T	18.	F	28.	$250
9.	T	19.	T	29.	$294
10.	T	20.	T	30.	10%

TEST 4

DIRECTIONS: Each question or incomplete statement is followed by several suggested answers or completions. Select the one that BEST answers the question or completes the statement. *PRINT THE LETTER OF THE CORRECT ANSWER IN THE SPACE AT THE RIGHT.*

Questions 1-12.

DIRECTIONS: Each of Questions 1 through 12 consists of a statement. You are to indicate whether the statement is TRUE (T) or FALSE (F). *PRINT THE LETTER OF THE CORRECT ANSWER IN THE SPACE AT THE RIGHT.*

1. The supplies used during a fiscal period are shown on the balance sheet as a current asset. 1.____

2. If the assets and liabilities increase equally, the proprietorship also increases. 2.____

3. The Income and Expense Statement shows the results of business operations over a period of time. 3.____

4. An exchange of one asset for another asset of different value causes a change in the proprietorship. 4.____

5. The recording of allowance for depreciation actually results in writing down the asset values. 5.____

6. If the closing merchandise inventory is understated, the profit for the period will be understated. 6.____

7. If accrued salaries during a period are not recorded, the profit for the period will be overstated. 7.____

8. If sales returns are understated during a fiscal period, the profit for that period will be understated. 8.____

9. Unpaid salaries should be added to the salaries for the period before the profit for the period is figured. 9.____

10. When posting the Sales Journal, each item is posted separately to the accounts receivable controlling account in the General Ledger. 10.____

11. A business is said to be solvent when it has a net profit for the period. 11.____

12. Accrued income is income earned but not received during a fiscal period. 12.____

Questions 13-30.

DIRECTIONS: Below is a list of terms with an accompanying list of definitions or explanations. In the space at the right, put the letter of the term in Column II which BEST explains the definition or explanation in Column I.

COLUMN I

COLUMN II

13. Entries needed to bring accounts up to date at the end of an accounting period

14. An entry in a book of original entry that has more than one debit or credit

15. An account used to summarize the income and expense data at the close of the fiscal period

16. An account with a balance that is partly a balance sheet amount and partly an income statement amount

17. Discount granted to a customer for early payment of his account

18. A journal designed for recording a particular type of transaction only

19. A ledger used for recording the details of a single account

20. An account in the general ledger that is supported by a subsidiary ledger

21. A list of individual account balances in a subsidiary ledger

22. Expense items bought and paid for, but not entirely consumed during the fiscal period

23. Expenses incurred but not paid during a fiscal period

24. The decrease in the value of a fixed asset due to wear and tear

25. The amount of unsold merchandise on hand

A. Abstract
B. Accrued expenses
C. Adjusting entries
D. Allowance for bad debts
E. Book value
F. Cash discount
G. Compound entry
H. Controlling account
I. Current asset
J. Depreciation
K. Fixed asset
L. General ledger
M. Income & expense summary
N. Merchandise inventory
O. Mixed account
P. Petty cash
Q. Prepaid expenses
R. Retail method
S. Special journal
T. Straight-line method
U. Subsidiary ledger
V. Voucher

13.____
14.____
15.____
16.____
17.____
18.____
19.____
20.____
21.____
22.____
23.____
24.____
25.____

26. Assets of a more or less permanent nature used in the business   26._____

27. The amount of estimated uncollectible accounts receivable.   27._____

28. The most commonly used method of computing depreciation   28._____

29. The difference between the original cost of an asset and its valuation amount   29._____

30. A written authorization required for each expenditure   30._____

KEY (CORRECT ANSWERS)

1.	F	11.	F	21.	A
2.	F	12.	T	22.	Q
3.	T	13.	C	23.	B
4.	T	14.	G	24.	J
5.	F	15.	M	25.	N
6.	T	16.	O	26.	K
7.	T	17.	F	27.	D
8.	F	18.	S	28.	T
9.	T	19.	U	29.	E
10.	F	20.	H	30.	V

TEST 5

Questions 1-12.

DIRECTIONS: Questions 1 through 12 are to be answered by writing the CORRECT amount in the space at the right.

1. If the purchases for the month were $500, the beginning inventory was $1,500, the ending inventory was $1,000, and the gross profit was $2,000, what were the sales? 1.____

2. If the gross profit for the period was $750 and the net profit was $250, what was the amount of the expenses? 2.____

3. Determine the amount of the cost of goods sold if the purchases for the month were $10,000, the beginning inventory was $3,000, and the ending inventory was $5,000. 3.____

4. A typewriter was purchased for $300 with an estimated life of five years. What is the book value at the end of the third year? 4.____

5. A delivery truck costs $3,000. Its book value at the end of the third year was $2,100. What is the amount of depreciation each year? 5.____

6. The assets on a Balance Sheet are $7,500. The liabilities are $4,500. What is the capital? 6.____

7. A check was received for $242.50 in payment of a sale amounting to $250 less discount. What is the percent of discount allowed? 7.____

8. The capital at the close of the fiscal period was $10,000. The liabilities were $12,000. What are the TOTAL assets? 8.____

9. A note is dated March 1 and is due in 60 days. What is its due date? 9.____

10. A note is dated January 30. It is due in one month. What is its due date? 10.____

11. What is the interest on a note for $500 with interest at 6% for sixty days? 11.____

12. What is the interest on a note for $800 with interest at 6% for 45 days? 12.____

Questions 13-15

DIRECTIONS: Each of Questions 13 through 25 consists of a statement. You are to indicate whether the statement is TRUE (T) or FALSE (F). *PRINT THE LETTER OF THE CORRECT ANSWER IN THE SPACE AT THE RIGHT.*

13. To determine the value of the merchandise available for sale, the purchases are added to the beginning merchandise inventory. 13.____

14. The closing merchandise inventory is shown on both the Balance Sheet and the Income and Expense Statement.   14.____

15. The allowance for bad debts account is closed into the income and expense summary account at the close of the fiscal period.   15.____

16. The accounts payable account shows the total amount owed to creditors and also shows how much is owed to each creditor.   16.____

17. Sales discount is usually subtracted from the sales in the Income and Expense Statement.   17.____

18. The use of controlling accounts increases the possibility of errors in preparing the trial balance.   18.____

19. The use of controlling accounts results in fewer accounts in the General Ledger.   19.____

20. The total of the schedule of accounts receivable should equal the balance of the accounts receivable account in the General Ledger.   20.____

21. Closing entries summarize in the income and expense summary account the income costs and expense for the fiscal period.   21.____

22. The post-closing trial balance is made before the Balance Sheet has been made.   22.____

23. The closing entries are recorded in the General Journal.   23.____

24. The debit balance of the equipment account should show the book value of the equipment on hand.   24.____

25. The balance of the allowance for depreciation of equipment account is shown on the Balance Sheet.   25.____

KEY (CORRECT ANSWERS)

1.	$3,000		11.	$5.00
2.	$500		12.	$6.00
3.	$8,000		13.	T
4.	$120		14.	T
5.	$300		15.	F
6.	$3,000		16.	F
7.	3%		17.	T
8.	$22,000		18.	F
9.	April 30		19.	T
10.	Feb. 28		20.	T

21. T
22. F
23. T
24. F
25. T

EXAMINATION SECTION
TEST 1

DIRECTIONS: Each question or incomplete statement is followed by several suggested answers or completions. Select the one that BEST answers the question or completes the statement. *PRINT THE LETTER OF THE CORRECT ANSWER IN THE SPACE AT THE RIGHT.*

Questions 1-5.

DIRECTIONS: Questions 1 through 5 are to be answered on the basis of the statement account shown below.

STATEMENT OF ACCOUNT

Regal Tools, Inc.
136 Culver Street
Cranston, R.I. 02910

TO: Vista, Inc.
     572 No. Copeland Ave.
     Pawtucket, R.I. 02800

DATE: March 31

DATE	ITEM	CHARGES	PAYMENTS AND CREDITS	BALANCE
	Previous Balance			785.35
March 8	Payment		785.35	----
12	Invoice 17-582	550 --		550.00
17	Invoice 17-692	700 --		1250.00
31	Payment		550.00	700.00

PAY LAST AMOUNT SHOWN IN BALANCE COLUMN

1. Which company is the customer?   1.____

2. What total amount was charged by the customer during March?   2.____

3. How much does the customer owe on March 31?   3.____

4. On which accounting schedule would Vista list Regal?   4.____

5. The terms on invoice 17-582 were 3/20, n/45.
What was the CORRECT amount for which the check should have been written when payment was made?   5.____

31

2 (#1)

6. Which item is NOT a source document? A(n)

   A. invoice
   B. magnetic tape
   C. punched card
   D. telephone conversation

7. What is double-entry accounting?

   A. Journalizing and posting
   B. Recording debit and credit parts for a transaction
   C. Using carbon paper when preparing a source document
   D. Posting a debit or credit and computing the new account balance

8. The balance in the asset account Supplies is $600. An ending inventory shows $200 of supplies on hand.
   The adjusting entry should be

   A. debit Supplies Expense for $200, credit Supplies for $200
   B. credit Supplies Expense for $200, debit Supplies for $200
   C. debit Supplies Expense for $400, credit Supplies for $400
   D. credit Supplies Expense for $400, debit Supplies for $400

9. What is the purpose of preparing an Income Statement? To

   A. report the net income or net loss
   B. show the owner's claims against the assets
   C. prove that the accounting equation is in balance
   D. prove that the total debits equal the total credits

10. Which account does NOT belong on the Income Statement?

    A. Salaries Payable
    B. Rental Revenue
    C. Advertising Expense
    D. Sales Returns and Allowances

11. The source document for entries made in a Purchases Journal is a purchase

    A. order   B. requisition   C. invoice   D. register

12. A business check guaranteed for payment by the bank is called a

    A. bank draft
    B. certified check
    C. cashier's check
    D. personal check

13. The entry that closes the Purchases Account contains a

    A. debit to Purchases
    B. debit to Purchases Returns and Allowances
    C. credit to Purchases
    D. credit to Income and Expense Summary

14. Which account would NOT appear on a Balance Sheet?

    A. Office Equipment
    B. Transportation In
    C. Mortgage Payable
    D. Supplies on Hand

15. Which entry is made at the end of the fiscal period for the purpose of updating the Prepaid Insurance Account? _____ entry.

    A. Correcting   B. Closing   C. Adjusting   D. Reversing

16. Which deduction from gross pay is NOT required by law?

    A. Hospitalization insurance
    B. FICA tax
    C. Federal income tax
    D. New York State income tax

17. What is the last date on which a 2 percent cash discount can be taken for an invoice dated October 15 with terms of 2/10, n/30?

    A. October 15
    B. October 17
    C. October 25
    D. November 14

18. Which item on the bank reconciliation statement would require the business to record a journal entry?
    A(n)

    A. deposit in transit
    B. outstanding check
    C. canceled check
    D. bank service charge

19. Which is NOT an essential component of a computer?
    A(n)

    A. input device
    B. central processor
    C. output device
    D. telecommunicator

20. Which group of accounts could appear on a post-closing trial balance?

    A. Petty Cash; Accounts Receivable; FICA Taxes Payable
    B. Office Furniture; Office Expense; Supplies on Hand
    C. Supplies Expense; Sales; Advertising Expense
    D. Sales Discount; Rent Expense; J. Smith, Drawing

21. The withdrawals of cash by the owner are recorded in the owner's drawing account as a(n)

    A. adjusting entry
    B. closing entry
    C. credit
    D. debit

22. An account in the General Ledger which shows a total of a related Subsidiary Ledger is referred to as a(n) _____ account.

    A. revenue
    B. controlling
    C. temporary
    D. owner's equity

23.

> *For Deposit Only*
> *Anthony Gill*

Which type of endorsement is shown above?

A. Restrictive B. Blank
C. Full D. Qualified

24. Which is a chronological record of all the transactions of a business?

A. Worksheet B. Income Statement
C. Journal D. Trial balance

25. Which error would NOT be revealed by the preparation of a trial balance?

A. Posting of an entire transaction more than once
B. Incorrectly pencil footing the balance of a general ledger account
C. Posting a debit of $320 as $230
D. Omitting an account with a balance

26. The Cash Receipts Journal is used to record the

A. purchase of merchandise for cash
B. purchase of merchandise on credit
C. sale of merchandise for cash
D. sale of merchandise on credit

27. On a systems flowchart, which symbol is commonly used to indicate the direction of the flow of work? A(n)

A. arrow B. circle C. diamond D. rectangle

28. Which account balance would be eliminated by a closing entry at the end of the fiscal period?

A. Office Equipment B. Owner's Drawing
C. Owner's Capital D. Mortgage Payable

29. In a data processing system, the handling and manipulation of data according to precise procedures is called

A. input B. processing
C. storage D. output

30. Which financial statement reflects the cumulative financial position of the business?

A. Bank statement B. Income statement
C. Trial balance D. Balance sheet

31. Which account should be credited when recording a cash proof showing an overage? 31._____

    A. Sales
    B. Cash
    C. Cash Short and Over
    D. Sales Returns and Allowances

32. In which section of the income statement would the purchases account be shown? 32._____

    A. Cost of Goods Sold
    B. Income from Sales
    C. Operating Expenses
    D. Other Expenses

33. What is an invoice? 33._____
    A(n)

    A. order for the shipment of goods
    B. order for the purchase of goods
    C. receipt for goods purchased
    D. statement listing goods purchased

34. A business uses a Sales Journal, a Purchases Journal, a Cash Receipts Journal, a Cash Payments Journal, and a General Journal. 34._____
    In which journal would a credit memorandum received from a creditor be recorded?
    _____ Journal

    A. Sales
    B. Purchases
    C. General
    D. Cash Receipts

35. Which account is debited to record a weekly payroll? 35._____

    A. Employees Income Tax Payable
    B. FICA Taxes Payable
    C. General Expense
    D. Salaries Expense

KEY (CORRECT ANSWERS)

1. Vista, Inc.
2. $1,250
3. $700
4. Accts. Payable
5. $533.50

6. D
7. B
8. C
9. A
10. A

11. C
12. B
13. C
14. D
15. C

16. A
17. C
18. D
19. D
20. A

21. D
22. B
23. A
24. C
25. A

26. C
27. A
28. B
29. B
30. D

31. C
32. A
33. D
34. C
35. D

EXAMINATION SECTION

TEST 1

DIRECTIONS: Each question or incomplete statement is followed by several suggested answers or completions. Select the one that BEST answers the question or completes the statement. *PRINT THE LETTER OF THE CORRECT ANSWER IN THE SPACE AT THE RIGHT.*

Questions 1-5.

DIRECTIONS: Questions 1 through 5 are to be answered on the basis of the extracts from Federal income tax withholding and Social Security tax tables shown below. These tables indicate the amounts which must be withheld from the employee's salary by his employer for Federal income tax and for Social Security. They are based on weekly earnings.

INCOME TAX WITHHOLDING TABLE							
The wages are		And the number of withholding allowances is					
At Least	But Less Than	5	6	7	8	9	10 or More
^^	^^	The amount of income tax to be withheld shall be					
$300	$320	$24.60	$19.00	$13.80	$ 8.60	$4.00	$ 0
320	340	28.80	22.80	17.40	12.20	7.00	2.80
340	360	33.00	27.00	21.00	15.80	10.60	5.60
360	380	37.20	31.20	25.20	19.40	14.20	9.00
380	400	41.40	34.40	29.40	23.40	17.80	12.60
400	420	45.60	39.60	33.60	27.60	21.40	16.20
420	440	49.80	43.80	37.80	31.80	25.60	19.80
440	460	54.00	48.00	42.00	36.00	29.80	23.80
460	480	58.20	52.20	46.20	40.20	34.00	38.00
480	500	62.40	46.40	40.40	44.40	38.20	32.20

SOCIAL SECURITY TABLE					
WAGES		Tax to be Withheld	WAGES		Tax to be Withheld
At Least	But Less Than	^^	At Least	But Less Than	^^
$333.18	$333.52	$19.50	$336.60	$336.94	$19.70
333.52	333.86	19.52	336.94	337.28	19.72
333.86	334.20	19.54	337.28	337.62	19.74
334.20	334.54	19.56	337.62	337.96	19.76
334.54	334.88	19.58	337.96	338.30	19.78
334.88	335.22	19.60	338.30	338.64	19.80
335.22	335.56	19.62	338.64	338.98	19.82
335.56	335.90	19.64	338.98	339.32	19.84
335.90	336.24	19.66	339.32	339.66	19.86
336.24	336.60	19.68	339.66	340.00	19.88

1. If an employee has a weekly wage of $379.50 and claims 6 withholding allowances, the amount of income tax to be withheld is
    A. $27.00   B. $31.20   C. $35.40   D. $37.20

2. An employee had wages of $335.60 for one week. With eight withholding allowances claimed, how much income tax will be withheld from his salary?
    A. $8.60   B. $12.00   C. $13.80   D. $17.40

3. How much social security tax will an employee with weekly wages of $335.60 pay?
    A. $19.60   B. $19.62   C. $19.64   D. $19.66

4. Mr. Wise earns $339.80 a week and claims seven withholding allowances. What is his take-home pay after income tax and social security tax are deducted?
    A. $300.32   B. $302.52   C. $319.92   D. $322.40

5. If an employee pays $19.74 in social security tax and claims eight withholding allowances, the amount of income tax that should be withheld from his wages is
    A. $8.60   B. $12.20   C. $13.80   D. $15.80

6. A fundamental rule of bookkeeping states that an individual's assets equal his liabilities plus his proprietorship (ASSETS = LIABILITIES − PROPRIETORSHIP). Which of the following statements logically follows from this rule?
    A. ASSETS = PROPRIETORSHIP − LIABILITIES
    B. LIABILITIES = ASSETS + PROPRIETORSHIP
    C. PROPRIETORSHIP = ASSETS − LIABILITIES
    D. PROPRIETORSHIP = LIABILITIES + ASSETS

7. Mr. Martin's assets consist of the following:
    Cash on Hand: $5,233.74
    Furniture: $4,925.00
    Government Bonds: $5,500.00
    What are his TOTAL assets?
    A. $10,158.74   B. $10,425.00   C. $10,733.74   D. $15,658.74

8. If Mr. Mitchell has $627.04 in his checking account and then writes three checks for $241.74, $13.24, and $101.97, what will be his new balance?
    A. $257.88   B. $269.08   C. $357.96   D. $368.96

9. An employee's net pay is equal to his total earnings less all deductions. If an employee's total earnings in a pay period are $497.05, what is his NET pay if he has the following deductions: Federal income tax, $90.32; FICA: $28.74; State tax: $18.79; City tax: $7.25; Pension: $1.88?
    A. $351.17   B. $351.07   C. $350.17   D. $350.07

10. A petty cash fund had an opening balance of $85.75 on December 1.   10.____
Expenditures of $23.00, $15.65, $5.23, $14.75, and $26.38 were made out of his fund during the first 14 days of the month. Then, on December 17, another $38.50 was added to the fund.
If additional expenditures of $17.18, $3.29, and $11.64 were made during the remainder of the month, what was the FINAL balance of the petty cash fund at the end of December?
   A. $6.93   B. $7.13   C. $46.51   D. $91.40

Questions 11-15.

DIRECTIONS: Questions 11 through 15 are to be answered on the basis of the following instructions.

The chart below is used by the loan division of a city retirement system for the following purposes: (1) to calculate the monthly payment a member must pay on an outstanding loan; (2) to calculate how much a member owes on an outstanding loan after he has made a number of payments.

To calculate the amount a member must pay each month in repaying his loan, look at Column II on the chart. You will notice that each entry in Column II corresponds to a number appearing under the *Months* column; for example, 1.004868 corresponds to 1 month, 0.503654 corresponds to 2 months, etc. To calculate the amount a member must pay each month, use the following procedure: multiply the amount of the load by the entry in Column II which corresponds to the number of months over which the load will be paid back. For example, if a loan of $200 is taken out for six months, multiply $200 by 0.169518, the entry in Column II which corresponds to six months.

In order to calculate the balance still owed on an outstanding loan, multiply the monthly payment by the number in Column I which corresponds to the number of monthly payments which remain to be paid on the loan. For example, if a member is supposed to pay $106.00 a month for twelve months, after seven payments, five monthly payments remain. To calculate the balance owed on the loan at this point, multiply the $106.00 monthly payment by 4.927807, the number in Column I that corresponds to five months.

Months	Column I	Column II
1	0.995156	1.004868
2	1.985491	0.503654
3	2.971029	0.336584
4	3.951793	0.253050
5	4.927807	0.202930
6	5.899092	0.169518
7	6.865673	0.145652
8	7.827572	0.127754
9	8.784811	0.113833
10	9.737414	0.102697
11	10.685402	0.093586
12	11.628798	0.085994
13	12.567624	0.079570
14	13.501902	0.074064
15	14.431655	0.069292

11. If Mr. Carson borrows $1,500 for eight months, how much will he have to pay back each month?
    A. $187.16   B. $191.63   C. $208.72   D. $218.65

12. If a member borrows $2,400 for one year, the amount he will have to pay back each month is
    A. $118.78   B. $196.18   C. $202.28   D. $206.38

13. Mr. Elliott borrowed $1,700 for a period of fifteen months. Each month he will have to pay back
    A. $117.80   B. $116.96   C. $107.79   D. $101.79

14. Mr. Aylward is paying back a thirteen-month loan at the rate of $173.13 a month.
    If he has already made six monthly payments, how much does he owe on the outstanding loan?
    A. $1,027.38   B. $1,178.75   C. $1,188.65   D. $1,898.85

15. A loan was taken out for 15 months, and the monthly payment was $104.75. After two monthly payments, how much was still owed on this load?
    A. $515.79   B. $863.89   C. $1,116.76   D. $1,316.46

16. The ABC Corporation had a gross income of $125,500.00 in 2015. Of this, it paid 60% for overhead.
    If the gross income for 2016 increased by $6,500 and the cost of overhead increased to 61% of gross income, how much more did it pay for overhead in 2016 than in 2015?
    A. $1,320   B. $5,220   C. $7,530   D. $8,052

5 (#1)

17. After one year, Mr. Richards paid back a total of $1,695.00 as payment for a $1,500.00 loan. All the money paid over $1,500.00 was simple interest. The interest charge was MOST NEARLY
    A. 13%   B. 11%   C. 9%   D. 7%

    17._____

18. A checking account has a balance of $253.36.
    If deposits of $36.95, $210.23, and $7.34 and withdrawals of $117.35, $23.37, and $15.98 are made, what is the NEW balance of the account?
    A. $155.54   B. $351.18   C. $364.58   D. $664.58

    18._____

19. In 2015, the W Realty Company spent 27% of its income on rent.
    If it earned $97,254.00 in 2015, the amount it paid for rent was
    A. $26.258.58   B. $26,348.58   C. $27,248.58   D. $27,358.58

    19._____

20. Six percent simple annual interest on $2,436.18 is MOST NEARLY
    A. $145.08   B. $145.17   c. $146.08   D. $146.17

    20._____

21. Assume that the XYZ Company has $10,402.72 cash on hand.
    If it pays $699.83 of this for rent, the amount of cash on hand would be
    A. $9,792.89   B. $9,702.89   C. $9,692.89   D. $9,602.89

    21._____

22. On January 31, Mr. Warren's checking account had a balance of $933.68.
    If he deposited $36.40 on February 2, $126.00 on February 9, and $90.02 on February 16 and wrote no checks during this period, what was the balance of his account on February 17?
    A. $680.26   B. $681.26   C. $1,186.10   D. $1,187.00

    22._____

23. Multiplying a number by .75 is the same as
    A. multiplying it by 2/3
    B. dividing it by 2/3
    C. multiplying it by 3/4
    D. dividing it by 3/4

    23._____

24. In City Agency A, 2/3 of the employees are enrolled in a retirement system. City Agency B has the same number of employees as Agency A, and 60% of these are enrolled in a retirement system.
    If Agency A has a total of 660 employees, how many MORE employees does it have enrolled in a retirement system than does Agency B?
    B. 36   B. 44   C. 56   D. 66

    24._____

25. Net Worth is equal to Assets minus Liabilities.
    If, at the end of year, a textile company had assets of $98,695.83 and liabilities of $59,238.29, what was its net worth?
    A. $38,478.54   B. $38,488.64   C. $39,457.54   D. $48,557.54

    25._____

KEY (CORRECT ANSWERS)

1. B
2. B
3. C
4. B
5. B

6. C
7. D
8. B
9. D
10. B

11. B
12. D
13. A
14. C
15. D

16. B
17. A
18. B
19. A
20. D

21. B
22. C
23. C
24. B
25. C

TEST 2

DIRECTIONS: Each question or incomplete statement is followed by several suggested answers or completions. Select the one that BEST answers the question or completes the statement. *PRINT THE LETTER OF THE CORRECT ANSWER IN THE SPACE AT THE RIGHT.*

Questions 1-10.

DIRECTIONS: Questions 1 through 10 below present the identification numbers, initials, and last names of employees enrolled in a city retirement system. You are to choose the option (A, B, C, or D) that has the IDENTICAL identification number, initials, and last name as those given in each question.

<u>Sample Question</u>
B145698 JL Jones
  A. B146798 JL Jones   B. B145698 JL Jonas
  C. P145698 JL Jones   D. B145698 JL Jones

The correct answer is D. Only Option D shows the identification number, initials, and last name exactly as they are in the sample question. Options A, B, and C have errors in the identification number or last name.

1. J297483 PL Robinson
 A. J294783 PL Robinson   B. J297483 PL Robinson
 C. J297483 Pl Robinson   D. J297843 PL Robinson

2. S497662 JG Schwartz
 B. S497662 JG Schwarz   B. S497762 JG Schwartz
 C. S497662 JG Schwartz   D. S497663 JG Schwartz

3. G696436 LN Alberton
 A. G696436 LM Alberton   B. G696436 LN Albertson
 C. G696346 LN Albertson   D. G696436 LN Alberton

4. R774923 AD Aldrich
 A. R774923 AD Aldrich   B. R744923 AD Aldrich
 C. R774932 AP Aldrich   D. R774932 AD Allrich

5. N239638 RP Hrynyk
 A. N236938 PR Hrynyk   B. N236938 RP Hrynyk
 C. N239638 PR Hrynyk   D. N239638 Hrynyk

6. R156949 LT Carlson
 A. R156949 LT Carlton   B. R156494 LT Carlson
 C. R159649 LT Carlton   D. R156949 LT Carlson

7. T524697 MN Orenstein
 A. T524697 MN Orenstein   B. T524967 MN Orinstein
 C. T524697 NM Ornstein   D. T524967 NM Orenstein

8. L346239 JD Remsen
   A. L346239 JD Remson
   B. L364239 JD Remsen
   C. L346329 JD Remsen
   D. L346239 JD Remsen

9. P966438 SB Rieperson
   A. P996438 SB Rieperson
   B. P466438 SB Reiperson
   C. R996438 SB Rieperson
   D. P966438 SB Rieperson

10. D749382 CD Thompson
    A. P749382 CD Thompson
    B. D749832 CD Thomsonn
    C. D749382 CD Thompson
    D. D749823 CD Thomspon

Questions 11-20.

DIRECTIONS: Assume that each of the capital letters in the table below represents the name of an employee enrolled in the city's employees' personnel system. The number directly beneath the letter represents the agency for which the employee works, and the small letter directly beneath represents the code for the employee's account.

Name of Employee	L	O	T	Q	A	M	R	N	C
Agency	3	4	5	9	8	7	2	1	6
Account Code	r	f	b	i	d	t	g	e	n

In each of the following Questions 11 through 20, the agency code numbers and the account code letters in Columns 2 and 3 should correspond to the capital letters in Column 1 and should be in the same consecutive order. For each question, look at each column carefully and mark your answer as follows:

If there are one or more errors in Column 2 only, mark your answer A.
If there are one or more errors in Column 3 only, mark your answer B.
I there are one or more errors in Column 2 and one or more errors in Column 3, mark your answer C.
If there are NO errors in either column, mark your answer D.

Sample Question

Column 1	Column 2	Column 3
TQLMOC	583746	birtfn

In Column 2, the second agency code number (corresponding to letter Q) should be 9, not 8. Column 3 is coded correctly to Column 1. Since there is an error only in Column 2, the correct answer is A.

3 (#2)

	COLUMN 1	COLUMN 2	COLUMN 3	
11.	QLNRCA	931268	iregnd	11.___
12.	NRMOTC	127546	egftbn	12.___
13.	RCTALM	265837	gndbrt	13.___
14.	TAMLON	578341	bdtrfe	14.___
15.	ANTORM	815427	debigt	15.___
16.	MRALON	728341	tgdrfe	16.___
17.	CTNQRO	657924	ndeigf	17.___
18.	QMROTA	972458	itgfbd	18.___
19.	RQMCOL	297463	gitnfr	19.___
20.	NOMRTQ	147259	eftgbi	20.___

Questions 21-25.

DIRECTIONS: Questions 21 through 25 are to be answered SOLELY on the basis of the following passage.

The city may issue its own bonds or it may purchase bonds as an investment. Bonds may be issued in various denominations, and the face value of the bond is its par value. Before purchasing a bond, the investor desires to know the rate of income that the investment may yield in computing the yield on a bond, it is assumed that the investor will keep the bond until the date of maturity, except for callable bonds which are not considered in this passage. To compute exact yield is a complicated mathematical problem, and scientifically prepared tables are generally used to avoid such computation. However, the approximate yield can be computed much more easily. In computing approximate yield, the accrued interest on the date of purchase should be ignored because the buyer who pays accrued interest to the seller receives it again at the next interest date. Bonds bought at a premium (which cost more) yield a lower rate of income than the same bonds bought at par (face value), and bounds bought at a discount (which cost less) yield a higher rate of income than the same bonds bought at par.

21. An investor bought a $10,000 city bond paying 6% interest. 21.___
    Which of the following purchase prices would indicate that the bond was bought at a premium?
    A. $9,000   B. $9,400   C. $10,000   D. $10,600

22. During 2016, a particular $10,000 bond paying 7 ½% sold at fluctuating prices. 22.___
    Which of the following prices would indicate that the bond was bought at a discount?
    A. $9,800   B. $10,000   C. $10,200   D. $10,750

45

23. A certain group of bonds was sold in denominations of $5,000, $10,000, $20,000, and $50,000.
In the following list of four purchase prices, which one is MOST likely to represent a bond sold at par value?
  A. $10,500   B. $20,000   C. $22,000   D. $49,000

24. When computing the approximate yield on a bond, it is DESIRABLE to
  A. assume the bond was purchased at par
  B. consult scientifically prepared tables
  C. ignore accrued interest on the date of purchase
  D. wait until the bond reaches maturity

25. Which of the following is MOST likely to be an exception to the information provided in the above passage?
Bonds
  A. purchased at a premium
  B. sold at par
  C. sold before maturity
  D. which are callable

KEY (CORRECT ANSWERS)

1.	B		11.	D
2.	C		12.	C
3.	D		13.	B
4.	A		14.	A
5.	D		15.	B
6.	D		16.	D
7.	A		17.	C
8.	D		18.	D
9.	D		19.	A
10.	C		20.	D

21. D
22. A
23. B
24. C
25. D

TEST 3

DIRECTIONS: Each question or incomplete statement is followed by several suggested answers or completions. Select the one that BEST answers the question or completes the statement. *PRINT THE LETTER OF THE CORRECT ANSWER IN THE SPACE AT THE RIGHT.*

Questions 1-6.

DIRECTIONS: Questions 1 through 6 consist of computations of addition, subtraction, multiplication, and division. For each question, do the computation indicated, and choose the correct answer from the four choices given.

1. ADD: 8936
7821
8953
4297
9785
6579

   A. 45371   B. 45381   C. 46371   D. 46381

2. SUBTRACT: 95,432
67,596

   A. 27,836   B. 27,846   C. 27,936   D. 27,946

3. MULTIPLY: 987
867

   A. 854609   B. 854729   C. 855709   D. 855729

4. DIVIDE: $59\overline{)321439.0}$

   A. 5438.1   B. 5447.1   C. 5448.1   D. 5457.1

5. DIVIDE: $.057\overline{)721}$

   A. 12,648.0   B. 12,648.1   C. 12,649.0   D. 12,649.1

6. ADD: 1/2 + 5/7
   A. 1 3/14   B. 1 2/7   C. 1 5/14   D. 1 3/7

7. If the total number of employees in one city agency increased from 1,927 to 2,006 during a certain year, the percentage increase in the number of employees for that year is MOST NEARLY
   A. 4%   B. 5%   C. 6%   D. 7%

8. During a single fiscal year, which totaled 248 workdays, one account clerk verified 1,488 purchase vouchers.
   Assuming a normal work week of five days, what is the average number of vouchers verified by the account clerk in a one-week period during this fiscal year?
   A. 25   B. 30   C. 35   D. 40

8.____

9. If the city department of purchase bought 190 computers for $793.50 each and 208 computers for $839.90 each, the TOTAL price paid for these computers is
   A. $315,813.00   B. $325,464.20
   C. $334,279.20   D. $335,863.00

9.____

Questions 10-14.

DIRECTIONS: Questions 10 through 14 are to be answered SOLELY on the basis of the information given in the following paragraph.

   Since discounts are in common use in the commercial world and apply to purchases made by government agencies as well as business firms, it is essential that individuals in both public and private employment who prepare bills, check invoices, prepare payment vouchers, or write checks to pay bills have an understanding of the terms used. These include cash or time discount, trade discount, and disconnect series. A cash or time discount offers a reduction in price to the buyer for the prompt payment of the bill and is usually expressed as a percentage with a time requirement, stated in days, within which the bill must be paid in order to earn the discount. An example would be 3/10, meaning a 3% discount may be applied to the bill if the payment is forwarded to the vendor within ten days. On an invoice, the cash discount terms are usually followed by the net terms, which is the time in days allowed for ordinary payment of the bill. Thus, 3/10, Net 30 means that full payment is expected in thirty days if the cash discount of 3% is not taken for having paid the bill within ten days. When the expression Terms Net Cash is listed on a bill, it means that no deduction for early payment is allowed. A trade discount is normally applied to list prices by a manufacturer to show the actual price to retailers so that they may know their cost and determine markups that will allow them to operate competitively and at a profit. A trade discount is applied by the seller to the list price and is independent of a cash or time discount. Discounts may also be used by manufacturers to adjust prices charged to retailers without changing list prices. This is usually done by series discounting and is expressed as a series of percentages. To compute a series discount, such as 40%, 20%, 10%, first apply the 40% discount to the list price, then apply the 20% discount to the remainder, and finally apply the 10% discount to the second remainder.

10. According to the above passage, trade discounts are
    A. applied by the buyer   B. independent of cash discounts
    C. restricted to cash sales   D. used to secure rapid payment of bills

10.____

11. According to the above passage, if the sales terms 5/10, Net 60 appear on a bill in the amount of $100 dated December 5, 2016 and the buyer submits his payment on December 15, 2016, his PROPER payment should be
    A. $60   B. $90   C. $95   D. $100

11.____

12. According to the above passage, if a manufacturer gives a trade discount of 40% for an item with a list price of $250 and the terms are Net Cash, the price a retail merchant is required to pay for this item is 12.____
    A. $250   B. $210   C. $150   D. $100

13. According to the above passage, a series discount of 25%, 20%, 10% applied to a list price of $200 results in an ACTUAL price to the buyer of 13.____
    A. $88   B. $90   C. $108   D. $110

14. According to the above passage, if a manufacturer gives a trade discount of 50% and the terms are 6/10, Net 30, the cost to a retail merchant of an item with a list price of $500 and for which he takes the time discount is 14.____
    A. $220   B. $235   C. $240   D. $250

Questions 15-22.

DIRECTIONS: Questions 15 through 22 each show in Column I the information written on five cards (lettered j, k, l, m, n) which have to be filed. You are to choose the option (lettered A, B, C, or D) in Column II which BEST represents the proper order of filing according to the information, rules, and sample question given below.

A file card record is kept of the work assignments for all the employees in a certain bureau. On each card is the employee's name, the date of work assignment, and the work assignment code number. The cards are to be filed according to the following rules:

FIRST: File in alphabetical order according to employee's name.

SECOND: When two or more cards have the same employee's name, file according to the assignment date, beginning with the earliest date.

THIRD: When two or more cards have the same employee's name and the same date, file according to the work assignment number beginning with the lowest number.

Column II shows the cards arranged in four different orders. Pick the option (A, B, C, or D) in Column II which shows the correct arrangement of the cards according to th above filing rules.

SAMPLE QUESTION

Column I
j. Cluney 4/8/02 (486503)
k. Roster 5/10/01 (246611)
l. Altool 10/15/02 (711433)
m. Cluney 12/18/02 (527610)
n. Cluney 4/8/02 (486500)

Column II
A. k, l, m, j, n
B. k, n, j, l, m
C. l, k, j, m, n
D. l, n, j, m, k

The correct way to file the cards is:
- l. Altool 10/15/02 (71143)
- n. Cluney 4/8/02 (486500)
- j. Cluney 4/8/02 (486503)
- m. Cluney 12/18/02 (527610)
- k. Roster 5/10/01 (246611)

The correct filing order is shown by the letters l, n, j, m, k. The answer to the sample question is the letter D, which appears in front of the letters l, n, j, m, k in Column II.

COLUMN I   COLUMN II

15. j. Smith 3/19/03 (662118)   A. j, m, l, n, k   15._____
     k. Turner 4/16/99 (481349)   B. j, l, n, m, k
     l. Terman 3/20/02 (210229)   C. k, n, m, l, j
     m. Smyth 3/20/02 (481359)   D. j, n, k, l, m
     n. Terry 5/11/01 (672128)

16. j. Ross 5/29/02 (396118)   A. l, m, k, n, j   16._____
     k. Rosner 5/29/02 (439281)   B. m, l, k, n, j
     l. Rose 7/19/02 (723456)   C. l, m, k, j, n
     m. Rosen 5/29/03 (829692)   D. m, l, j, n, k
     n. Ross 5/29/02 (399118)

17. j. Sherd 10/12/99 (552368)   A. n, m, k, j, l   17._____
     k. Snyder 11/12/99 (539286)   B. j, m, l, k, n
     l. Shindler 10/13/98 (426798)   C. m, k, n, j. l
     m. Scherld 10/12/99 (552386)   D. m, n, j, l, k
     n. Schneider 11/12/99 (798213)

18. j. Carter 1/16/02 (489636)   A. k, n, j, l, m   18._____
     k. Carson 2/16/01 (392671)   B. n, k, m, l, j
     l. Carter 1/16/01 (486936)   C. n, k, l, j, m
     m. Carton 3/15/00 (489639)   D. k, n, l, j, m
     n. Carson 2/16/01 (392617)

19. j. Thomas 3/18/99 (763182)   A. m, l, j, k, n   19._____
     k. Tompkins 3/19/00 (928439)   B. j, m, l, k, n
     l. Thomson 3/21/00 (763812)   C. j, l, n, m, k
     m. Thompson 3/18/99 (924893)   D. l, m, j, n, k
     n. Tompson 3/19/99 (928793)

20. j. Breit 8/10/03 (345612)   A. m, j, n, k, l   20._____
     k. Briet 5/21/00 (837543)   B. n, m, j, k, l
     l. Bright 9/18/99 (931827)   C. m, j, k, l, n
     m. Breit 3/7/98 (553984)   D. j, m, k, l, n
     n. Brent 6/14/04 (682731)

5 (#3)

COLUMN I   COLUMN II

21. j. Roberts 10/19/02 (581932)   A. n, k, l, m, j   21._____
     k. Rogers 8/9/00 (638763)   B. n, k, l, j, m
     l. Rogerts 7/15/97 (105689)   C. k, n, l, m, j
     m. Robin 3/8/92 (287915)   D. j, m, k, n, l
     n. Rogers 4/2/04 (736921)

22. j. Hebert 4/28/02 (719468)   A. n, k, j, m, l   22._____
     k. Herbert 5/8/01 (938432)   B. j, l, n, k, m
     l. Helbert 9/23/04 (832912)   C. l, j, k, n, m
     m. Herbst 7/10/03 (648599)   D. l, j, n, k, m
     n. Herbert 5/8/01 (487627)

23. In order to pay its employees, the Convex Company obtained bills and coins   23._____
    in the following denominations:

Denomination	$20	$10	$5	$1	$.50	$.25	$.10	$.05	$.01
Number	317	122	38	73	69	47	39	25	36

    What was the TOTAL amount of cash obtained?
       A. $7,874.76   B. $7,878.00   C. $7,889.25   D. $7,924.35

24. H. Partridge receives a weekly gross salary (before deductions) of $596.25.   24._____
    Through weekly payroll deductions of $19.77, he is paying back a load he took
    from his pension fund.
    If other fixed weekly deductions amount to $184.14, how much pay would Mr.
    Partridge take home over a period of 33 weeks?
       A. $11,446.92   B. $12,375.69   C. $12,947.22   D. $19,676.25

25. Mr. Robertson is a city employee enrolled in a city retirement system. He has   25._____
    taken out a loan from the retirement fund and is paying it back at the rate of
    $14.90 every two weeks.
    In eighteen weeks, how much money will he have paid back on the loan?
       A. $268.20   B. $152.80   C. $124.10   D. $67.05

26. In 2015, the Iridor Book Company had the following expenses: rent, $6,500;   26._____
    overhead, $52,585; inventory, $35,700, and miscellaneous, $1,275.
    If all of these expenses went up 18% in 2016, what would they TOTAL in 2016?
       A. $17,290.80   B. $78,768.20   C. $96,060.00   D. $113,350.80

27. Ms. Ranier had a gross salary of $355.36, paid once every week.   27._____
    If the deductions from each paycheck are $62.72, $25.13, $6.29, and $1,27, how
    much money would Ms. Ranier take home in four weeks?
       A. $1,039.80   B. $1,421.44   C. $2,079.60   D. $2,842.88

28. Mr. Martin had a net income of $19,100 for the year. 28.____
If he spent 34% on rent and household expenses, 3% on house furnishings, 25% on clothes, and 36% on food, how much was left for savings and other expenses?
    A. $196.00   B. $382.00   C. $649.40   D. $1,960.00

29. Mr. Elsberg can pay back a loan of $1,800 from the city employees' retirement 29.____
system if he pays back $36.69 every two weeks for two full years.
At the end of the two years, how much more than the original $1,800 he borrowed will Mr. Elsberg have paid back?
    A. $53.94   B. $107.88   C. $190.79   D. $214.76

30. Mrs. Nusbaum is a city employee, receiving a gross salary (salary before 30.____
deductions) of $31,200. Every two weeks, the following deductions are taken out of her salary: Federal Income Tax, $243.96; FICA, $66.39; State Tax, $44.58; City Tax, $20.91; Health Insurance, $4.71.
If Mrs. Nusbaum's salary and deductions remained the same for a full calendar year, what would her NET salary (gross salary less deductions) be in that year?
    A. $9,894.30   B. $21,305.70   C. $28,118.25   D. $30,819.45

KEY (CORRECT ANSWERS)

1.	C	11.	C	21.	D		
2.	A	12.	C	22.	B		
3.	D	13.	C	33.	A		
4.	C	14.	B	24.	C		
5.	D	15.	A	25.	C		
6.	A	16.	C	26.	D		
7.	A	17.	D	27.	A		
8.	B	18.	C	28.	B		
9.	B	19.	B	29.	B		
10.	B	20.	A	30.	B		

EXAMINATION SECTION
TEST 1

DIRECTIONS: Each question or incomplete statement is followed by several suggested answers or completions. Select the one that BEST answers the question or completes the statement. *PRINT THE LETTER OF THE CORRECT ANSWER IN THE SPACE AT THE RIGHT.*

1. In the preparation of a balance sheet, failure to consider the inventory of office supplies will result in _____ assets and _____. 1.____

   A. overstating; overstating liabilities
   B. understating; overstating capital
   C. understating; understating capital
   D. overstating; understating liabilities

2. The annual federal unemployment tax is paid by the 2.____

   A. employer *only*
   B. employee *only*
   C. employer and the employee equally
   D. employee, up to a maximum of 30 cents per week, and the balance is paid by the employer

3. Which are NORMALLY considered as current assets? 3.____

   A. Bank overdrafts   B. Prepaid expenses
   C. Accrued expenses   D. Payroll taxes

4. What type of ledger account is a summary of a number of accounts in another ledger? The _____ account. 4.____

   A. controlling   B. subsidiary
   C. asset   D. proprietorship

5. The PRIMARY purpose of a petty cash fund is to 5.____

   A. provide a fund for paying all miscellaneous expenses
   B. take the place of the cash account
   C. provide a common drawing fund for the owners of the business
   D. avoid entering a number of small amounts in the Cash Payments Journal

6. In the absence of a written agreement, profits in a partnership would be divided 6.____

   A. in proportion to the investment of the partners
   B. on an equitable basis depending on the time and effort spent by the partners
   C. equally
   D. on a ratio of investment basis, giving the senior partner preference

7. Which account represents a subtraction or decrease to an income account? 7.____

   A. Purchase Returns & Allowances
   B. Sales Returns & Allowances
   C. Freight In
   D. Prepaid Rent

8. If the Interest Expense account showed a debit balance of $210 as of December 31, and $40 of this amount was prepaid on Notes Payable, which statement is CORRECT as of December 31?

   A. Prepaid Interest of $170 should be shown as a deferred expense in the balance sheet.
   B. Interest Expense should be shown in the Income Statement as $210.
   C. Prepaid Interest of $40 should be listed as a deferred credit to income in the balance sheet.
   D. Interest Expense should be shown in the Income Statement as $170.

9. When prices are rising, which inventory-valuation method results in the LOWEST inventory value?

   A. FIFO
   B. LIFO
   C. Average cost
   D. Declining balance

10. Which of the following is a CORRECT procedure in preparing a bank reconciliation?

    A. Deposits in transit should be added to the cash balance on the books, and outstanding checks should be deducted from the cash balance on the bank statement.
    B. The cash balance on the bank statement and the cash balance on the books should be equal if there are deposits in transit and outstanding checks.
    C. Outstanding checks should be deducted from the cash balance on the books.
    D. Any service charge should be deducted from the check stub balance.

11. Which ratio indicates that there may NOT be enough on hand to meet current obligations?

    A. $\dfrac{\text{fixed assets}}{\text{fixed liabilities}} = \dfrac{2}{3}$
    B. $\dfrac{\text{total assets}}{\text{total obligations}} = \dfrac{3}{5}$
    C. $\dfrac{\text{current assets}}{\text{current liabilities}} = \dfrac{1}{3}$
    D. $\dfrac{\text{current assets}}{\text{fixed liabilities}} = \dfrac{1}{2}$

12. Which asset is NOT subject to depreciation?

    A. Factory equipment
    B. Land
    C. Buildings
    D. Machinery

13. Which form is prepared to verify that the total of the account balances in the Customers Ledger agrees with the balance in the controlling account in the General Ledger?

    A. Worksheet
    B. Schedule of accounts payable
    C. Schedule of accounts receivable
    D. Trial balance

14. If the merchandise inventory on hand at the end of the year was overstated, what will be the result of this error?   14._____

    A. *Understatement* of income for the year
    B. *Overstatement* of income for the year
    C. *Understatement* of assets at the end of the year
    D. No effect on income or assets

15. Working capital is found by subtracting the total current liabilities from the total   15._____

    A. fixed liabilities   B. fixed assets
    C. current income   D. current assets

16. Which is the CORRECT procedure for calculating the rate of merchandise turnover?   16._____

    A. Gross Sales divided by Net Sales
    B. Cost of Sales divided by Average Inventory
    C. Net Purchases divided by Average Inventory
    D. Gross Purchases divided by Net Purchases

17. The books of the Atlas Cement Corporation show a net profit of $142,000. To close the Profit and Loss account of the corporation at the end of the year, the account CREDITED should be   17._____

    A. Earned Surplus   B. Capital Stock
    C. C. Atlas, Capital   D. C. Atlas, Personal

18. The bank statement at the end of the month indicated a bank charge for printing a new checkbook.   18._____
    How is this information recorded?
    Debit

    A. Cash and credit Office Supplies
    B. Office Supplies and credit the Bank Charges
    C. the Bank Charges and credit Office Supplies
    D. Miscellaneous Expense and credit Cash

19. The Allowance for Doubtful Accounts appears on the balance sheet as a deduction from   19._____

    A. Accounts Receivable   B. Notes Receivable
    C. Accounts Payable   D. Notes Payable

20. The Tucker Equipment Corporation had a $45,000 profit for the year ended December 31.   20._____
    Which would be the PROPER entry to close the Income and Expense account at the end of the year?
    Debit Income and Expense Summary; credit

    A. Tucker, Capital   B. Tucker, Drawing
    C. Retained Earnings   D. Capital Stock

21. A failure to record a purchases invoice would be discovered when the

    A. monthly statement of account is sent to the customer
    B. check is received from the customer
    C. check is sent to the creditor
    D. statement of account is received from the creditor

22. Which General Ledger account would appear in a post-closing trial balance?

    A. Notes Receivable
    B. Bad Debts Expense
    C. Sales Discount
    D. Fee Income

23. Which deduction is affected by the number of exemptions claimed?

    A. State Disability
    B. State income tax
    C. FICA tax
    D. Workers' Compensation

24. The face value of a 60-day, 12% promissory note is $900. The maturity value of this note will be

    A. $909   B. $900   C. $918   D. $1,008

25. An invoice dated March 10, terms 2/10, n/30, should be paid no later than

    A. March 20   B. March 31   C. April 9   D. April 10

KEY (CORRECT ANSWERS)

1. C
2. A
3. B
4. A
5. D
6. C
7. B
8. D
9. B
10. D

11. C
12. B
13. C
14. B
15. D
16. B
17. A
18. D
19. A
20. C

21. D
22. A
23. B
24. C
25. C

TEST 2

DIRECTIONS: Each question or incomplete statement is followed by several suggested answers or completions. Select the one that BEST answers the question or completes the statement. *PRINT THE LETTER OF THE CORRECT ANSWER IN THE SPACE AT THE RIGHT.*

1. Which is NOT an essential element of a computer system?

   A. Input
   C. Verifier
   B. Central processing unit
   D. Output

2. The general ledger account that would NOT appear in a post-closing trial balance would be

   A. Cash
   C. Furniture and Fixtures
   B. Accounts Payable
   D. Sales Income

3. Ralph Hanley, age 45, supports his wife and three children. Mr. Hanley is the only member of the family required to file an income tax return. What is the MAXIMUM number of exemptions he can claim?

   A. One   B. Five   C. Three   D. Four

4. The cost of a fixed asset minus the allowance for depreciation (accumulated depreciation) is the _____ value.

   A. market   B. cost   C. liquidation   D. book

5. The form used by a bookkeeper in summarizing adjustments and information which will be used in preparing statements is called a

   A. journal
   C. ledger
   B. balance sheet
   D. worksheet

6. When a large number of transactions of a particular kind are to be entered in bookkeeping records, it is USUALLY advisable to use

   A. cash records
   C. special journals
   B. controlling accounts
   D. special ledgers

7. The petty cash book shows a petty cash balance of $9.80 on May 31. The petty cash box contains only $9.10. What account will be debited to record the $.70 difference?

   A. Cash
   C. Cash Short and Over
   B. Petty Cash
   D. Petty Cash Expense

8. The ONLY difference between the books of a partnership and those of a sole proprietorship appears in the _____ accounts.

   A. proprietorship
   C. asset
   B. liability
   D. expense

9. The earnings of a corporation are FIRST recorded as a credit to an account called

   A. Dividends Payable
   C. Retained Earnings
   B. Capital Stock Authorized
   D. Profit and Loss Summary

10. A firm purchased a new delivery truck for $2,900 and sold it four years later for $500. The Allowance for Depreciation of Delivery Equipment account was credited for $580 at the end of each of the four years.
    When the machine was sold, there was a

    A. loss of $80
    B. loss of $1,820
    C. loss of $2,400
    D. gain of $80

11. FICA taxes are paid by

    A. employees *only*
    B. employers *only*
    C. both employees and employers
    D. neither employees nor employers

12. Which phase of the data processing cycle is the SAME as calculating net pay in a manual system?

    A. Input   B. Processing   C. Storing   D. Output

13. Which error will cause the trial balance to be out of balance?

    A. A sales invoice for $60 was entered in the Sales Journal for $600.
    B. A credit to office furniture in the journal was posted as a credit to office machines in the ledger.
    C. A debit to advertising expense in the journal was posted as a debit to miscellaneous expense in the ledger.
    D. A debit to office equipment in the journal was posted as a credit to office equipment in the ledger.

14. The collection of a bad debt previously written off will result in a(n)

    A. *decrease* in assets
    B. *decrease* in capital
    C. *increase* in assets
    D. *increase* in liabilities

15. Which account does NOT belong in the group?

    A. Notes Receivable
    B. Building
    C. Office Equipment
    D. Delivery Truck

16. The adjusting entry to record the estimated bad debts is debit _____ and credit _____.

    A. Allowance for Bad Debts; Bad Debts Expense
    B. Bad Debts Expense; Allowance for Bad Debts
    C. Allowance for Bad Debts; Accounts Receivable
    D. Bad Debts Expense; Accounts Receivable

17. At the end of the year, which account should be closed into the income and expense summary?

    A. Freight In
    B. Allowance for Doubtful Accounts
    C. Notes Receivable
    D. Petty Cash

18. Which form is prepared to aid in verifying that the customer's account balances in the customer's ledger agree with the balance in the Accounts Receivable account in the general ledger?

    A. Worksheet
    B. Schedule of Accounts Payable
    C. Schedule of Accounts Receivable
    D. Trial Balance

19. In the preparation of an income statement, failure to consider accrued wages will result in

    A. *overstating* operating expense and understating net profit
    B. *overstating* net profit *only*
    C. *understating* operating expense and overstating net profit
    D. *understating* operating expense *only*

20. The CORRECT formula for determining the rate of merchandise turnover is

    A. cost of goods sold divided by average inventory
    B. net sales divided by net purchases
    C. gross sales divided by ending inventory
    D. average inventory divided by cost of goods sold

21. A legal characteristic of a corporation is _____ liability.

    A. contingent   B. limited
    C. unlimited   D. deferred

22. A customer's check you had deposited is returned to you by the bank labeled *Dishonored*.
    What entries would be made as a result of this action? Debit _____ and credit _____.

    A. cash; customer's account
    B. miscellaneous expense; cash
    C. customer's account; capital
    D. customer's account; cash

23. The TOTAL capital of a corporation may be found by adding

    A. assets and liabilities
    B. assets and capital stock
    C. liabilities and capital stock
    D. earned surplus and capital stock

24. The source of an entry made in the Petty Cash book is the

    A. general ledger   B. voucher
    C. register   D. general journal

25. Which account is debited to record interest earned but not yet due?

    A. Deferred Interest
    B. Interest Receivable
    C. Interest Income
    D. Income and Expense Summary

KEY (CORRECT ANSWERS)

1. C
2. D
3. B
4. D
5. D

6. C
7. C
8. A
9. C
10. A

11. C
12. B
13. D
14. C
15. A

16. B
17. A
18. C
19. C
20. A

21. B
22. D
23. D
24. B
25. B

TEST 3

DIRECTIONS: Each question or incomplete statement is followed by several suggested answers or completions. Select the one that BEST answers the question or completes the statement. *PRINT THE LETTER OF THE CORRECT ANSWER IN THE SPACE AT THE RIGHT.*

1. Which reason should NOT generally be used by an employer when making a hiring decision?
   An applicant('s)

   A. resume reveals a lack of job-related skills
   B. attendance record on a previous job is poor
   C. has improperly prepared the job application
   D. is married

   1._____

2. Graves, Owens, and Smith formed a partnership and invested $15,000 each. If the firm made a profit of $18,000 last year and profits and losses were shared equally, what was Owens' share of the net profit?

   A. $1,000   B. $5,000   C. $6,000   D. $9,000

   2._____

3. The bank statement balance of the Bedford Co. on May 31 was $3,263.28. The checkbook balance was $3,119.06. A reconciliation showed that the outstanding checks totaled $147.22 and that there was a bank service charge of $3.00. The CORRECT checkbook balance should be

   A. $3,260.28   B. $3,122.06   C. $3,116.06   D. $3,266.28

   3._____

4. Which account is shown in a post-closing trial balance?

   A. Prepaid Insurance   B. Fees Income
   C. Purchases   D. Freight In

   4._____

5. A check endorsed *For deposit only (signed) Samuel Jones* is an example of a _____ endorsement.

   A. full   B. blank   C. complete   D. restrictive

   5._____

6. The selling price of a share of stock as published in a daily newspaper is called the _____ value.

   A. book   B. face   C. par   D. market

   6._____

7. Which is obtained by dividing the cost of goods sold by the average inventory?

   A. Current ratio
   B. Merchandise inventory turnover
   C. Average rate of mark-up
   D. Acid-test ratio

   7._____

8. A Suzuki truck costing $39,000 is expected to have a useful life of six years and a salvage value of $3,000.
   If $6,000 is debited to the depreciation expense account each year for six years, what method of depreciation is used?

   A. Units of production   B. Straight line
   C. Declining balance   D. Sum of the years digits

   8._____

61

9. Which form is prepared to aid in verifying that the customer's account balances in the customer's ledger agree with the balance in the Accounts Receivable account in the General Ledger?

   A. Worksheet
   B. Schedule of Accounts Payable
   C. Schedule of Accounts Receivable
   D. Trial Balance

10. In the preparation of a balance sheet, failure to consider commissions owed to salespersons will result in _____ liabilities and _____ capital.

    A. understating; overstating
    B. understating; understating
    C. overstating; overstating
    D. overstating; understating

11. A financial statement generated by a computer is an example of a(n)

    A. audit trail
    B. output
    C. input
    D. program

12. Merchandise was sold for $150 cash plus a 3% sales tax. The CORRECT credit(s) should be

    A. Sales Income $150, Sales Taxes Payable $4.50
    B. Sales Income $154.50
    C. Merchandise $150, Sales Taxes Payable $4.50
    D. Sales Income $150

13. The bookkeeper should prepare a bank reconciliation MAINLY to determine

    A. which checks are outstanding
    B. whether the checkbook balance and the bank statement balance are in agreement
    C. the total amount of checks written during the month
    D. the total amount of cash deposited during the month

14. Which is the CORRECT procedure for calculating the rate of merchandise turnover?

    A. Gross Sales divided by Net Sales
    B. Cost of Goods Sold divided by Average Inventory
    C. Net Purchases divided by Average Inventory
    D. Gross Purchases divided by Net Purchases

15. Which previous job should be listed FIRST on a job application form? The

    A. least recent job
    B. most recent job
    C. job you liked best
    D. job which paid the most

16. Failure to record cash sales will result in

    A. *overstatement* of profit
    B. *understatement* of profit
    C. *understatement* of liabilities
    D. *overstatement* of capital

17. When a fixed asset is repaired, the cost of the repairs should be _____ account.

    A. *debited* to the asset
    B. *debited* to the expense
    C. *credited* to the proprietor's capital
    D. *credited* to the asset

18. The form used by a bookkeeper to summarize information which will be used in preparing financial statements is called a

    A. journal
    B. balance sheet
    C. ledger
    D. worksheet

19. Which type of ledger account is a summary of a number of accounts in another ledger? _____ account.

    A. Controlling
    B. Subsidiary
    C. Asset
    D. Proprietorship

20. What is the summary entry on the Purchases Journal?
    Debit _____ and credit _____.

    A. Accounts Payable; Merchandise Purchases
    B. Accounts Receivable; Merchandise Purchases
    C. Merchandise Purchases; Accounts Receivable
    D. Merchandise Purchases; Accounts Payable

21. The source document for entries made in the Sales Journal is a(n)

    A. credit memo
    B. statement of accounts
    C. invoice
    D. bill of lading

22. A Trial Balance which is in balance would NOT reveal the

    A. omission of the credit part of an entry
    B. posting of the same debit twice
    C. omission of an entire transaction
    D. omission of an account with a balance

23. A financial statement prepared by a computerized accounting system is an example of

    A. input
    B. output
    C. flowcharting
    D. programming

24. The form which the payroll clerk gives to each employee to show gross earnings and taxes withheld for the year is a

    A. W-2   B. W-3   C. W-4   D. 1040

25. Who would be the LEAST appropriate reference on an application for a job?
    A

    A. relative
    B. guidance counselor
    C. former employer
    D. prominent member of the community

KEY (CORRECT ANSWERS)

1.	D	11.	B
2.	C	12.	A
3.	C	13.	B
4.	A	14.	B
5.	D	15.	B
6.	D	16.	B
7.	B	17.	B
8.	B	18.	D
9.	C	19.	A
10.	A	20.	D

21. C
22. C
23. B
24. A
25. A

EXAMINATION SECTION
TEST 1

DIRECTIONS: Each question or incomplete statement is followed by several suggested answers or completions. Select the one that BEST answers the question or completes the statement. *PRINT THE LETTER OF THE CORRECT ANSWER IN THE SPACE AT THE RIGHT.*

Questions 1-7.

DIRECTIONS: Questions 1 through 7 are to be answered on the basis of the following income statement.
    Laura Lee's Bridal Shop
    Income Statement
    For the Year Ended December 31, 2018

```
Revenue:
    New & Used Bridal Gowns & Accessories                        $55,000
Expenses:
    Advertisement Expense               $ 2,000
    Salaries Expense                     12,000
    Dry cleaning & Alterations           10,000
    Utilities                             1,500
    Total Expenses                                                25,500
Net Income                                                       $29,500
```

1. What is the period of time covered by this income statement?   1._____

   A. January-December 2017
   B. December 2018
   C. January 2017-December 2018
   D. January-December 2018

2. What is the source of the revenue?   2._____

   A. New and used bridal gowns, advertisements, salaries, dry cleaning, and utilities
   B. Advertisements, salaries, dry cleaning, alterations, and utilities
   C. New and used bridal gowns and accessories
   D. Net income

3. What is the total revenue?   3._____

   A. $25,500   B. $55,000   C. $29,500   D. $79,500

4. Which of the following are expenses?   4._____

   A. Salaries
   B. New and used bridal gowns and accessories
   C. Revenue
   D. New and used bridal gowns, advertisements, and dry cleaning

5. What are the total expenses?   5._____

   A. $55,000   B. $29,500   C. $79,500   D. $25,500

6. There is a resulting net income because 6.____

   A. total revenue and total expenses are combined
   B. net income is greater than total revenue
   C. the total revenue is greater than total expenses
   D. the total revenue is less than total expenses

7. Is this statement an interim statement? 7.____

   A. *Yes*, because it covers an entire accounting period
   B. *No*, because it covers an entire accounting period
   C. *Yes*, because it covers a period of less than a year
   D. *No*, because it covers a period of more than a year

8. What is the name of the accounting report that may show either a net profit or a net loss for an accounting period? 8.____

   A. Income statement   B. Balance sheet
   C. Statement of capital   D. Classified balance sheet

9. What are the two main parts of the body of the income statement? 9.____

   A. Cash and Capital   B. Revenue and Expenses
   C. Liabilities and Capital   D. Assets and Notes Payable

10. If total revenue exceeds total expenses for an accounting period, what is the difference called? 10.____

    A. Gross income   B. Total liabilities
    C. Total assets   D. Net income

11. In the body of a balance sheet, what are the three sections called? 11.____

    A. Assets and liabilities
    B. Cash, liabilities, and revenue
    C. Assets, liabilities, and capital
    D. Revenue, assets, and capital

12. What business record shows the results of the proprietor's borrowing assets from the business, usually in anticipation of profits? 12.____

    A. Proprietor's withdrawals
    B. Accounts payable
    C. Liabilities and Capital
    D. Total liabilities

Questions 13-24.

DIRECTIONS: For each transaction given for Mona's Magic Moments Hair Salon in Questions 13 through 24, identify which journal the transaction should be recorded in.

13. April 1: Mona, the owner, paid the month's rent - $600.00; check no. 356. 13.____

    A. General   B. Cash disbursements
    C. Purchases   D. Sales

14. April 6: the salon purchased $300.00 worth of styling products on account from Pomme de Terre Company. 14.____

    A. Cash disbursements B. General
    C. Sales D. Purchases

15. April 8: sold $100.00 worth of hair products on account to Mrs. Angela Bray. 15.____

    A. Sales B. Purchases
    C. Cash disbursements D. General

16. April 11: the owner, Mona Ramen, withdrew $80.00 of styling products for personal use. 16.____

    A. Sales B. Cash receipts
    C. General D. Cash disbursements

17. April 13: paid Pomme de Terre Company $300.00 on account; check 357. 17.____

    A. Purchases B. Cash disbursements
    C. Cash receipts D. General

18. April 15: cash sales to date were $4,607.00. 18.____

    A. Cash disbursements B. Purchases
    C. Sales D. General

19. April 17: issued credit slip #17 to Mrs. Angela Bray for $25.00 for merchandise returned. 19.____

    A. Cash disbursements B. Cash receipts
    C. Sales D. General

20. April 19: paid electric bill for $250.00; check no. 358. 20.____

    A. Cash disbursements B. Purchases
    C. General D. Cash receipts

21. April 21: received $75.00 from Mrs. Angela Bray for balance due on account. 21.____

    A. Sales B. Cash disbursements
    C. Cash receipts D. Purchases

22. April 23: sold $88.00 of hair products on account to Ms. Tania Alioto. 22.____

    A. Purchases B. Sales
    C. Cash disbursements D. Cash receipts

23. April 27: purchased $500.00 of equipment from Salon Stylings Merchandisers on account. 23.____

    A. Cash disbursements B. Sales
    C. General D. Purchases

24. April 30: cash sales to date were $5023.00. 24.____

    A. Purchases B. Sales
    C. Cash receipts D. General

Questions 25-30.

DIRECTIONS: Questions 25 through 30 are to be answered on the basis of the following ledger for a barbecue take-out restaurant owned and operated by Ruby Joiner.

Cash		Accounts Receivable		Delivery Equipment	
450	150	360	170	5,000	
212	125	250	100	4,000	
328	440	165	120	3,000	
172	125	100	60		
250	70				
275	150				
325	50				

Supplies		Ruby Joiner, Capital		Accounts Payable	
40			8,200	10	600
65			2,000	15	300
30			2,097		200
25					

Ruby Joiner, Drawing		Advertising Expense		Delivery Income	
225		40			400
175		45			350
200					250
					100

Trucking Expense		Telephone Expense	
100		80	
50		40	
		20	

25. What is the balance on the Cash account shown above?

    A. 2,012.00   B. 1,110.00   C. 3,122.00   D. 902.00

26. What is the balance on the Accounts receivable account shown above?

    A. 425.00   B. 875.00   C. 450.00   D. 1315.00

27. What is the balance on the Accounts payable account shown above?

    A. 1100.00   B. 1075.00   C. 25.00   D. 1125.00

28. Which of the above accounts has a balance of 1100.00?

    A. Accounts payable   B. Delivery Income
    C. Cash   D. Delivery equipment

29. Which of the above accounts has a balance of 12,000.00?

    A. Ruby Joiner, Capital
    B. Cash and Accounts receivable combined
    C. Delivery equipment
    D. None of the accounts

30. If you made a balance sheet out of the information listed above, Ruby Joiner's total assets would be

    A. 14,472.00   B. 12,297.00   C. 13,392.00   D. 13,487.00

Questions 31-34.

DIRECTIONS: Questions 31 through 34 are to be answered on the basis of the following information, to be included on a checking deposit ticket.

Five $20 bills; 11 $10 bills; 6 $5 bills; 47 $1 bills; 200 half dollars; 120 quarters; 112 dimes; 320 nickels; 67 pennies. Second National Bank (73-124) check of 152.34; Bank of the Midwest (13-298) check of 68.37; Great National Bank (32-165) check of 185.06.

31. What is the TOTAL currency for this deposit? 31.____
    A. $387   B. $287   C. $444.87   D. $157.87

32. What is the TOTAL coin for this deposit? 32.____
    A. $387   B. $287   C. $444.87   D. $157.87

33. What is the check total for this deposit? 33.____
    A. $692.77   B. $406   C. $405.77   D. $850.64

34. What is the TOTAL deposit? 34.____
    A. $444.87   B. $692.77   C. $851   D. $850.64

Questions 35-37.

DIRECTIONS: Questions 35 through 37 are to be answered on the basis of the following petty cash journal.

Date	Receipt No.	To Whom Paid	For What	Acct.#	Amount
10/2	1	Anna Jones - Mail	Postage	548	13.50
10/2	2	Jim Collins	Messenger	525	5.75
10/4	3	Anna Jones - Mail	Postage	548	13.50
10/5	4	Lucky Stores	Coffee	515	7.34
10/6	5	Tom Allen	Lunch w/customer	525	11.38

35. What is the TOTAL disbursement from this fund for the time period 10/1 through 10/6? 35.____
    A. $51.47   B. $40.09   C. $61.47   D. $26.59

36. How much money was disbursed to Account #548 during the time period 10/1-10/16? 36.____
    A. $51.47   B. $26   C. $27   D. $34.34

37. If the fund began the month with a total of $100.00, what amount was left in the fund at the end of business on 10/5? 37.____
    A. $48.53   B. $59.91   C. $51.47   D. $40.09

Questions 38-40.

DIRECTIONS: Questions 38 through 40 are to be answered on the basis of the following information.

A promissory note dated December 1, 2018, bearing interest at a rate of 12% and due in 90 days, is sent to a creditor. The face value of the note is $900.

38. What is the due date of the promissory note? 38.____

    A. January 15, 2019   B. March 1, 2019
    C. February 1, 2019   D. December 31, 2018

39. What is the TOTAL interest that will be earned on the note? 39.____

    A. $27   B. $270   C. $108   D. $10.80

40. What interest will be earned on the note for the old accounting period (December 1-31)? 40.____

    A. $90   B. $36   C. $9   D. $3.60

KEY (CORRECT ANSWERS)

1.	D	11.	C	21.	C	31.	B
2.	C	12.	A	22.	B	32.	D
3.	B	13.	B	23.	D	33.	C
4.	A	14.	D	24.	B	34.	D
5.	D	15.	A	25.	D	35.	A
6.	C	16.	C	26.	A	36.	C
7.	B	17.	B	27.	B	37.	B
8.	A	18.	C	28.	B	38.	B
9.	B	19.	D	29.	C	39.	A
10.	D	20.	A	30.	D	40.	C

TEST 2

DIRECTIONS: Each question or incomplete statement is followed by several suggested answers or completions. Select the one that BEST answers the question or completes the statement. *PRINT THE LETTER OF THE CORRECT ANSWER IN THE SPACE AT THE RIGHT.*

Questions 1-4.

DIRECTIONS: Questions 1 through 4 are to be answered on the basis of the following information, to be included in a deposit slip.

    14 twenty dollar bills   63 quarters
    52 ten dollar bills   22 dimes
    12 five dollar bills   44 nickels
    43 one dollar bills   70 pennies

Checks: $236.34 and $129.72

1. What is the TOTAL amount of currency for this deposit?   1.____
   A. $923.85   B. $1269.06   C. $903.00   D. $1299.91

2. What is the TOTAL amount of coin for this deposit?   2.____
   A. $20.85   B. $923.85   C. $903.00   D. $1299.91

3. What is the TOTAL amount of check for this deposit?   3.____
   A. $20.85   B. $366.06   C. $1299.91   D. $903.00

4. What is the TOTAL deposit for this slip?   4.____
   A. $1269.06   B. $903.00   C. $923.85   D. $1289.91

Questions 5-7.

DIRECTIONS: Questions 5 through 7 are to be answered on the basis of the following information.

Angela Martinez's last check stub balance was $675.50. Her bank statement balance dated April 30 was $652.00. A $250 deposit was in transit on that date. Outstanding checks were as follows: No. 127, $65.00; No. 129, $203.50; No. 130, $50.00. The bank service charge for the month was $5.00.

5. What was Angela Martinez's available checkbook balance on April 30?   5.____
   A. $652.00   B. $338.50   C. $583.50   D. $675.50

6. In order to reconcile her checkbook balance with her bank statement balance, what must Angela Martinez do?   6.____
       A. Add her checkbook balance to the balance on her bank statement
       B. Subtract her checkbook balance from the balance on her bank statement

C. Ignore her checkbook balance and adopt the balance on her bank statement
D. Adjust the checkbook balance by adding deposits and debiting outstanding checks and charges

7. The check stub balance referred to in the problem refers to the

   A. last check Angela Martinez recorded in her checkbook
   B. amount of money left in Angela Martinez's account according to her own calculations based on the checks, charges, and deposits she has written and recorded
   C. amount of money left in Angela Martinez's account according to the bank's calculations based on the checks, charges, and deposits posted to her account
   D. number of checks left in her checkbook

Questions 8-9.

DIRECTIONS: Questions 8 and 9 are to be answered on the basis of the following information.

Tu Nguyen, an interior designer, received his June bank statement on July 2. The balance was $622.66. His last check stub balance was $700. On comparing the two, he noticed that a deposit of $275 made on June 30 was not included on the statement; also, a bank service charge of $4 was deducted. Outstanding checks were as follows: No. 331, $97.50; No. 332, $207; No. 335, $25.40; and No. 336, $68.97.

8. What is Nguyen's CORRECT available bank balance?

   A. $494.79   B. $897.66   C. $700.00   D. $219.79

9. The bank statement balance referred to in the problem refers to the

   A. last check Tu Nguyen recorded in his checkbook
   B. last check presented for payment to Tu Nguyen's account
   C. amount of money left in Tu Nguyen's account according to the bank's calculations based on the checks, charges, and deposits posted to his account
   D. amount of money left in Tu Nguyen's account based on his own calculations of the checks, charges, and deposits he has written and recorded

10. What of the following endorsements would be an example of a simple Endorsement in Blank?

    A. Pay to the Order of Joanie Anderson
    B. Joanie Anderson
    C. For deposit only; Acct. No. 12345; Joanie Anderson
    D. Without Recourse; Joanie Anderson

11. Which of the following endorsements would limit the further purpose or use of the endorsed check?

    A. Pay to the Order of Joanie Anderson
    B. Joanie Anderson
    C. For deposit only; Acct. No. 12345; Joanie Anderson,
    D. Without Recourse; Joanie Anderson

12. Which of the following endorsements would protect the endorser from legal responsibility for payment, should the drawer have insufficient funds to honor his/her own check?

    A. Pay to the Order of Joanie Anderson
    B. Joanie Anderson
    C. For deposit only; Acct. No. 12345; Joanie Anderson
    D. Without Recourse; Joanie Anderson

Questions 13-24.

DIRECTIONS: Questions 13 - 24 are to be answered on the basis of the following ledger accounts for Wheelsmith Organic Farms.

Wheelsmith Organic Farms
Ledger Accounts

Cash	Accounts Payable	Service Supplies
Jan. 1	Jan. 1	Jan. 1
4,000	2,000	2,000

Shelley Wheelsmith, Capital	Machinery
Jan. 1	Jan. 1
11,000	7,000

13. Transaction #1: On January 5, Shelley Wheelsmith, the proprietor, received cash amounting to $5,000 as a result of returning machinery that had recently been purchased. What account(s) should this transaction be posted to?

    A. Cash
    B. Cash and Machinery
    C. Machinery
    D. Cash, Machinery, and Service Supplies

14. Transaction #2: On January 8, Shelley Wheelsmith, the proprietor, sent out a check for $600 in partial payment of the accounts payable.
    What account(s) should this transaction be posted to?

    A. Accounts Payable
    B. Accounts Payable and Cash
    C. Accounts Payable and Capital
    D. Cash

15. Transaction #3: On January 14, Shelley Wheelsmith, proprietor, made an additional investment in the business by contributing machinery valued at $1,500.
    What account(s) should this transaction be posted to?

    A. Machinery
    B. Machinery and Capital
    C. Capital
    D. Machinery and Cash

16. Transaction #4: On January 26, Shelley Wheelsmith, proprietor, purchased additional service supplies for $200. She agreed to pay the obligation in 30 days. What account(s) should this transaction be posted to?

A. Accounts Payable and Liabilities
B. Service supplies
C. Accounts Payable
D. Accounts Payable and Service supplies

17. Transaction #5: On January 31, Shelley Wheelsmith, proprietor, purchased service supplies paying cash of $50. What account(s) should this transaction be posted to?   17._____

    A. Service supplies
    B. Service supplies and Accounts Payable
    C. Cash and Service supplies
    D. Cash

18. What is the balance in the Cash account after all of these transactions are posted?   18._____

    A. $9,000   B. $1,000   C. $5,000   D. $8,350

19. What is the balance in the Machinery account after all of these transactions are posted?   19._____

    A. $7,000   B. $5,000   C. $3,500   D. $13,500

20. What is the balance in the Accounts Payable account after all of these transactions are posted?   20._____

    A. $800   B. $600   C. $2,600   D. $1,600

21. What is the balance in the Capital account after all of these transactions are posted?   21._____

    A. $12,500   B. $800   C. $11,600   D. $10,400

22. What is the balance in the Service supplies account after all of these transactions are posted?   22._____

    A. $2,000   B. $2,250   C. $750   D. $2,200

23. What are the total assets of Wheelsmith Organic Farms after these transactions have been posted?   23._____

    A. $10,600   B. $11,850   C. $14,100   D. $10,750

24. What are the total liabilities and capital for Wheelsmith Organic Farms after these transactions have been posted?   24._____

    A. $14,100   B. $12,500   C. $11,850   D. $10,600

Questions 25-28.

DIRECTIONS: Questions 25 through 28 are to be answered on the basis of the following information.

At the end of an accounting period, Andy's Framing Gallery recorded the following information: Sales, $125,225; Merchandise Inventory, December 31, $95,325; Purchases Returns and Allowances, $3,500; Merchandise Inventory, January 1, $98,725; Freight on Purchases, $2,500; Purchases, $120,000.

25. What are the net purchases for Andy's Framing Gallery during the accounting period? 25._____
   A. $120,000   B. $119,000   C. $3,500   D. $122,500

26. What is the cost of goods available for sale? 26._____
   A. $119,000   B. $98,725   C. $95,325   D. $217,725

27. What is the total cost of goods sold for this accounting period? 27._____
   A. $217,725   B. $95,325   C. $122,400   D. $125,225

28. What is the gross profit on sales for this accounting period? 28._____
   A. $2825   B. $2500   C. $125,225   D. $122,400

Questions 29-40.

DIRECTIONS: Questions 29 through 40 are to be answered on the basis of the following information.

The Joie de Vivre Co. received the promissory notes listed below during the last quarter of its calendar year:

	Date	Face Amount	Terms	Interest Rate	Date Discounted	Discount Rate
(1)	10/8	$3,600	30 days	-	10/18	9%
(2)	9/22	$8,000	60 days	6%	10/1	7%
(3)	11/15	$3,000	90 days	7%	11/20	8%

29. What is the due date for the first note? 29._____
   A. 12/31   B. 11/7   C. 12/7   D. 10/31

30. What interest will be due when the first note matures? 30._____
   A. $3   B. $3,600   C. $30   D. $0

31. What is the maturity value of the first note? 31._____
   A. $3,600   B. $3,630   C. $0   D. $3,603

32. What is the discount period for the first note? 32._____
   A. One fiscal year   B. 10 days
   C. 20 days   D. One month

33. What is the due date for the second note? 33._____
   A. 12/21   B. 11/21   C. 10/21   D. 1/21

34. What interest will be due when the second note matures? 34._____
   A. $60   B. $800.00   C. $8.00   D. $80.00

35. What is the maturity value of the second note? 35._____
   A. $8,000   B. $8,080   C. $8,800   D. $8,008

36. What is the discount period for the second note?
    A. 51 days   B. 10 days   C. 360 days   D. 60 days

37. What is the due date for the third note?
    A. 1/14   B. 12/15   C. 12/31   D. 2/13

38. What interest will be due when the third note matures?
    A. $5.25   B. $52.50   C. $525   D. $90

39. What is the maturity value of the third note?
    A. $3525   B. $3005.25   C. $3052.50   D. $3090

40. What is the discount period for the third note?
    A. 60 days   B. 85 days   C. 5 days   D. 90 days

KEY (CORRECT ANSWERS)

1.	C	11.	C	21.	A	31.	A
2.	A	12.	D	22.	B	32.	C
3.	B	13.	B	23.	C	33.	B
4.	D	14.	B	24.	A	34.	D
5.	C	15.	B	25.	B	35.	B
6.	D	16.	D	26.	D	36.	A
7.	B	17.	C	27.	C	37.	D
8.	A	18.	D	28.	A	38.	B
9.	C	19.	C	29.	B	39.	C
10.	B	20.	D	30.	D	40.	B

TEST 3

DIRECTIONS: Each question or incomplete statement is followed by several suggested answers or completions. Select the one that BEST answers the question or completes the statement. *PRINT THE LETTER OF THE CORRECT ANSWER IN THE SPACE AT THE RIGHT.*

Questions 1-8.

DIRECTIONS: Questions 1 through 8 are to be answered on the basis of the following Balance Sheet.

Laura Lee's Bridal Shop
Balance Sheet
December 31, 2018

Assets

Cash	$14,000	
Accounts Receivable	3,000	
Bridal Accessories	10,000	
Gowns and Other Inventory	30,000	
Total Assets		$57,000

Liabilities and Capital

Accounts Payable	$ 4,000	
Notes Payable	28,000	
Total Liabilities		$32,000
Laura Lee, Capital		25,000
Total Liabilities and Capital		$57,000

1. When was the balance sheet prepared? 1.____

   A. January 2019
   B. December 31, 2018
   C. After the close of the 2018 fiscal year
   D. December 1, 2018

2. How does the date on this balance sheet differ from the date on the statement of capital or income statement? 2.____

   A. It doesn't differ. The dates for each statement signify the same time period.
   B. The date on a balance sheet represents the period during which any changes indicated on the statement took place, whereas the other financial statements represent the moment in time when the statement was prepared.
   C. The date on a balance sheet represents the moment in time when the statement was prepared, whereas the other financial statements represent the period during which any changes indicated on the statement took place.
   D. The date on a balance sheet indicates an entire year, whereas the dates on the other statements indicate a single month.

3. Can Laura Lee purchase more bridal gowns for the business paying cash of $16,000? 3.____

   A. No, because the business has only $14,000 cash available
   B. Yes, because the business has $57,000 cash available
   C. Yes, because the business has $57,000 available in assets
   D. No, because the business has $57,000 in liabilities

77

4. What is the owner's equity of Laura Lee's Bridal Shop?
   Since total equity consists of total _____, total equity is _____.

   A. assets minus total liabilities and proprietor's capital; $0
   B. assets minus total liabilities; $25,000
   C. assets; $57,000
   D. liabilities and proprietor's capital; $57,000

5. What is the TOTAL amount of Laura Lee's claim against the total assets of the business?

   A. $57,000   B. $25,000   C. $0   D. $39,000

6. What is the amount of the creditors' claims against the assets of the business?

   A. $4,000   B. $57,000   C. $32,000   D. $28,000

7. What is the net income for the period?

   A. $57,000
   B. $0
   C. $25,000
   D. This information cannot be obtained from the balance sheet

8. What was the value of Laura Lee's ownership in this business on January 1, 2004?

   A. $25,000
   B. $57,000
   C. $14,000
   D. This information cannot be obtained from the balance sheet

Questions 9-21.

DIRECTIONS: Each of the transactions described in Questions 9 through 21 occurred within an accounting period. For each question, indicate which of the four journals the transaction would be recorded in.

9. Sale of goods on account

   A. Cash receipts   B. Cash payments
   C. General   D. Sales

10. Cash payment of a promissory note

    A. Cash payments   B. Cash receipts
    C. Sales   D. General

11. Received a credit memo from a creditor

    A. Purchases   B. General
    C. Sales   D. Cash payments

12. Sale of merchandise for cash

    A. Purchases   B. General
    C. Cash receipts   D. Cash payments

13. Received a check from a customer in partial payment of an oral agreement   13._____

    A. Purchases   B. Sales
    C. General   D. Cash receipts

14. Issued a credit memo to a customer   14._____

    A. Purchases   B. General
    C. Cash payments   D. Sales

15. Received a promissory note in place of an oral agreement from a customer   15._____

    A. General   B. Cash payments
    C. Cash receipts   D. Sales

16. Paid monthly rent   16._____

    A. General   B. Purchases
    C. Cash payments   D. Cash receipts

17. Sale of a service on credit   17._____

    A. Cash receipts   B. General
    C. Purchases   D. Sales

18. Purchase of office furniture on credit   18._____

    A. General   B. Purchases
    C. Cash payments   D. Cash receipts

19. Purchased merchandise for cash   19._____

    A. Cash payments   B. Cash receipts
    C. Sales   D. General

20. Cash refund to a customer   20._____

    A. Cash receipts   B. Sales
    C. General   D. Cash payments

21. Purchases made on credit   21._____

    A. Purchases   B. Sales
    C. Cash receipts   D. General

Questions 22-26.

DIRECTIONS: Questions 22 through 26 are to be answered on the basis of the following inventory, purchased by International Soap and Candle Traders, Inc.

700 units at $4.50, 320 units at $3.75, 550 units at $2.75, and 475 units at $1.90

22. Calculate the total price of the units that cost $4.50.   22._____

    A. $315   B. $31,500   C. $3,150   D. $2,800

23. Calculate the total price of the units that cost $3.75.   23._____

    A. $2062.50   B. $12,000   C. $120   D. $1,200

24. Calculate the total price of the units that cost $2.75.

    A. $1,512.50   B. $15,125   C. $151.25   D. $550

    24._____

25. Calculate the total price of the units that cost $1.90.

    A. $90.25   B. $9025   C. $902.50   D. $475

    25._____

26. Calculate the average cost per unit.

    A. $27   B. $33.10   C. $0.30   D. $3.31

    26._____

27. The interest on a promissory note is recorded at which of the following times?

    A. When the debt is incurred
    B. At the end of the accounting period
    C. When the note is paid
    D. At the beginning of each month

    27._____

28. The interest on a promissory note begins accruing at which of the following times?

    A. When the debt is incurred
    B. At the end of the accounting period
    C. When the note is paid
    D. At the beginning of each month

    28._____

29. The maturity value of an interest-bearing note is the

    A. interest accrued on the note plus a service charge imposed by the lender
    B. interest accrued on the note
    C. face value of the note
    D. principal of the note plus interest

    29._____

30. A cash receipts journal is used to record the

    A. number of cash sales a business makes
    B. number of credit sales a business makes
    C. collection of cash made by the business
    D. expenditure of cash made by the business

    30._____

31. Calculate the interest on a promissory note issued for $3,000 at an interest rate of 8%, due in 360 days. (Assume a banking year of 360 days.)

    A. $300   B. $240   C. $60   D. $360

    31._____

32. Calculate the total payment due for a promissory note issued for $1,000 at an interest rate of 10%, due in 90 days. (Assume a banking year of 360 days.)

    A. $25   B. $1050   C. $1000   D. $1025

    32._____

33. Calculate the total payment due for a promissory note issued for $5,000 at an interest rate of 6%, due in 60 days. (Assume a banking year of 360 days.)

    A. $5,050   B. $50   C. $5,000   D. $5,300

    33._____

34. Calculate the interest on a promissory note issued for $1,700 at an interest rate of 12%, due in 45 days. (Assume a banking year of 360 days.) 34._____

    A. $204   B. $1725.50   C. $25.50   D. $1904

35. Calculate the interest on a promissory note issued for $600 at an interest rate of 9%, due in 90 days. (Assume a banking year of 360 days.) 35._____

    A. $13.50   B. $135   C. $54   D. $540

KEY (CORRECT ANSWERS)

1. B		16. C	
2. C		17. D	
3. A		18. B	
4. B		19. A	
5. B		20. D	
6. C		21. A	
7. D		22. C	
8. D		23. D	
9. D		24. A	
10. A		25. C	
11. B		26. D	
12. C		27. C	
13. D		28. A	
14. B		29. D	
15. A		30. C	

31. B
32. D
33. A
34. C
35. A

RECORD KEEPING
EXAMINATION SECTION
TEST 1

DIRECTIONS: Each question or incomplete statement is followed by several suggested answers or completions. Select the one that BEST answers the question or completes the statement. *PRINT THE LETTER OF THE CORRECT ANSWER IN THE SPACE AT THE RIGHT.*

Questions 1-15.

DIRECTIONS: Questions 1 through 15 are to be answered on the basis of the following list of company names below. Arrange a file alphabetically, word-by-word, disregarding punctuation, conjunctions, and apostrophes. Then answer the questions.

    A Bee C Reading Materials
    ABCO Parts
    A Better Course for Test Preparation
    AAA Auto Parts Co.
    A-Z Auto Parts, Inc.
    Aabar Books
    Abbey, Joanne
    Boman-Sylvan Law Firm
    BMW Autowerks
    C Q Service Company
    Chappell-Murray, Inc.
    E&E Life Insurance
    Emcrisco
    Gigi Arts
    Gordon, Jon & Associates
    SOS Plumbing
    Schmidt, J.B. Co.

1. Which of these files should appear FIRST?   1.____
   A. ABCO Parts
   B. A Bee C Reading Materials
   C. A Better Course for Test Preparation
   D. AAA Auto Parts Co.

2. Which of these files should appear SECOND?   2.____
   A. A-Z Auto Parts, Inc.
   B. A Bee C Reading Materials
   C. A Better Course for Test Preparation
   D. AAA Auto Parts Co.

2 (#1)

3. Which of these files should appear THIRD? 3._____
   A. ABCO Parts   B. A Bee C Reading Materials
   C. Aabar Books   D. AAA Auto Parts Co.

4. Which of these files should appear FOURTH? 4._____
   A. Aabar Books   B. ABCO Parts
   C. Abbey, Joanne   D. AAA Auto Parts Co.

5. Which of these files should appear LAST? 5._____
   A. Gordon, Jon & Associates   B. Gigi Arts
   C. Schmidt, J.B. Co.   D. SOS Plumbing

6. Which of these files should appear between A-Z Auto Parts, Inc. and Abbey, Joanne? 6._____
   A. A Bee C Reading Materials
   B. AAA Auto Parts Co.
   C. ABCO Parts
   D. A Better Course for Test Preparation

7. Which of these files should appear between ABCO Parts and Aabar Books? 7._____
   A. A Bee C Reading Materials   B. Abbey, Joanne
   C. Aabar Books   D. A-Z Auto Parts

8. Which of these files should appear between Abbey, Joanne and Boman-Sylvan Law Firm? 8._____
   A. A Better Course for Test Preparation
   B. BMW Autowerks
   C. Chappell-Murray, Inc.
   D. Aabar Books

9. Which of these files should appear between Abbey, Joanne and C Q Service? 9._____
   A. A-Z Auto Parts, Inc.   B. BMW Autowerks
   C. Choices A and B   D. Chappell-Murray, Inc.

10. Which of these files should appear between C Q Service Company and Emcrisco? 10._____
    A. Chappell-Murray, Inc.   B. E&E Life Insurance
    C. Gigi Arts   D. Choices A and B

11. Which of these files should NOT appear between C Q Service Company and E&E Life Insurance? 11._____
    A. Gordon, Jon & Associates   B. Emcrisco
    C. Gigi Arts   D. All of the above

12. Which of these files should appear between Chappell-Murray, Inc. and   12.____
    Gigi Arts?
    A. C Q Service Inc., E&E Life Insurance, and Emcrisco
    B. Emcrisco, E&E Life Insurance, and Gordon, Jon & Associates
    C. E&E Life Insurance, and Emcrisco
    D. Emcrisco and Gordon, Jon & Associates

13. Which of these files should appear between Gordon, Jon & Associates and   13.____
    SOS Plumbing?
    A. Gigi Arts   B. Schmidt, J.B. Co.
    C. Choices A and B   D. None of the above

14. Each of the choices lists the four files in their proper alphabetical order   14.____
    EXCEPT
    A. E&E Life Insurance; Gigi Arts; Gordon, Jon & Associates; SOS Plumbing
    B. E&E Life Insurance; Emcrisco; Gigi Arts; SOS Plumbing
    C. Emcrisco; Gordon, Jon & Associates; SOS Plumbing; Schmidt, J.B. Co.
    D. Emcrisco; Gigi Arts; Gordon, Jon & Associates; SOS Plumbing

15. Which of the choices lists the four files in their proper alphabetical order?   15.____
    A. Gigi Arts; Gordon, Jon & Associates; SOS Plumbing; Schmidt, J.B. Co.
    B. Gordon, Jon & Associates; Gigi Arts; Schmidt, J.B. Co.; SOS Plumbing
    C. Gordon, Jon & Associates; Gigi Arts; SOS Plumbing; Schmidt, J.B. Co.
    D. Gigi Arts; Gordon, Jon & Associates; Schmidt, J.B. Co.; SOS Plumbing

16. The alphabetical filing order of two businesses with identical names is   16.____
    determined by the
    A. length of time each business has been operating
    B. addresses of the businesses
    C. last name of the company president
    D. no one of the above

17. In an alphabetical filing system, if a business name includes a number, it should   17.____
    be
    A. disregarded
    B. considered a number and placed at the end of an alphabetical section
    C. treated as though it were written in words and alphabetized accordingly
    D. considered a number and placed at the beginning of an alphabetical
       section

18. If a business name includes a contraction (such as *don't* or *it's*), how should   18.____
    that word be treated in an alphabetical system?
    A. Divide the word into its separate parts and treat it as two words
    B. Ignore the letters that come after the apostrophe
    C. Ignore the word that contains the contraction
    D. Ignore the apostrophe and consider all letters in the contraction

19. In what order should the parts of an address be considered when using an   19._____
    alphabetical filing system?
    A. City or town; state; street name; house or building number
    B. State; city or town; street name; house or building number
    C. House or building number; street name; city or town; state
    D. Street name; city or town; state

20. A business record should be cross-referenced when a(n)   20._____
    A. organization is known by an abbreviated name
    B. business has a name change because of a sale, incorporation, or other reason
    C. business is known by a *coined* or common name which differs from a dictionary spelling
    D. all of the above

21. A geographical filing system is MOST effective when   21._____
    A. location is more important than name
    B. many names or titles sound alike
    C. dealing with companies who have offices all over the world
    D. filing personal and business files

Questions 22-25.

DIRECTIONS: Questions 22 through 25 are to be answered on the basis of the list of items below, which are to be filed geographically. Organize the items geographically and then answer the questions.

   I. University Press at Berkeley, U.S.
   II. Maria Sanchez, Mexico City, Mexico
   III. Great Expectations Ltd. in London, England
   IV. Justice League, Cape Town, South Africa, Africa
   V. Crown Pearls Ltd. in London, England
   VI. Joseph Prasad in London, England

22. Which of the following arrangements of the items is composed according to the   22._____
    policy of: *Continent, Country, City, Firm or Individual Name*?
    A. V, III, IV, VI, II, I   B. IV, V, III, VI, II, I
    C. I, IV, V, III, VI, II   D. IV, V, III, VI, I, II

23. Which of the following files is arranged according to the policy of: 23._____
    Continent, Country, City, Firm or Individual Name?
    A. South Africa; Africa; Cape Town; Justice League
    B. Mexico; Mexico City; Maria Sanchez
    C. North America; United States; Berkeley; University Press
    D. England; Europe; London; Prasad, Joseph

5 (#1)

24. Which of the following arrangements of the items is composed according to the policy of: *Country, City, Firm or Individual Name*? 24.____
    A. V, VI, III, II, IV, I
    B. I, V, VI, III, II, IV
    C. VI, V, III, II, IV, I
    D. V, III, VI, II, IV, I

25. Which of the following files is arranged according to a policy of: *Country, City, Firm or Individual Name*? 25.____
    A. England; London; Crown Pearls Ltd.
    B. North America; United States; Berkeley; University Press
    C. Africa; Cape Town; Justice League
    D. Mexico City; Mexico; Maria Sanchez

26. Under which of the following circumstances would a phonetic filing system be MOST effective? 26.____
    A. When the person in charge of filing can't spell very well
    B. With large files with names that sound alike
    C. With large files with names that are spelled alike
    D. All of the above

Questions 27-29.

DIRECTIONS: Questions 27 through 29 are to be answered on the basis of the following list of numerical files.

     I.   391-023-100
     II. 361-132-170
     III. 385-732-200
     IV. 381-432-150
     V.   391-632-387
     VI. 361-423-303
     VII. 391-123-271

27. Which of the following arrangements of the files follows a consecutive-digit system? 27.____
    A. II, III, IV, I   B. I, V, VII, III   C. II, IV, III, I   D. III, I, V, VII

28. Which of the following arrangements follows a terminal-digit system? 28.____
    A. I, VII, II, IV, III
    B. II, I, IV, V, VII
    C. VII, VI, V, IV, III
    D. I, IV, II, III, VII

29. Which of the following lists follows a middle-digit system? 29.____
    A. I, VII, II, VI, IV, V, III
    B. I, II, VII, IV, VI, V, III
    C. VII, II, I, III, V, VI, IV
    D. VII, I, II, IV, VI, V, III

Questions 30-31.

DIRECTIONS: Questions 30 and 31 are to be answered on the basis of the following information.

  I. Reconfirm Laura Bates appointment with James Caldecort on December 12 at 9:30 A.M.
  II. Laurence Kinder contact Julia Lucas on August 3 and set up a meeting for week of September 23 at 4 P.M.
  III. John Lutz contact Larry Waverly on August 3 and set up appointment for September 23 at 9:30 A.M.
  IV. Call for tickets for Gerry Stanton August 21 for New Jersey on September 23, flight 143 at 4:43 P.M.

30. A chronological file for the above information would be 30.____
    A. IV, III, II, I   B. III, II, IV, I   C. IV, II, III, I   D. III, I, II, IV

31. Using the above information, a chronological file for the date September 23 would be 31.____
    A. II, III, IV   B. III, I, IV   C. III, II, IV   D. IV, III, II

Questions 32-34.

DIRECTIONS: Questions 32 through 34 are to be answered on the basis of the following information.

  I. Call Roger Epstein, Ashoke Naipaul, Jon Anderson, and Sara Washingon on April 19 at 1:00 P.M. to set up meeting with Alika D'Ornay for June 6 in New York.
  II. Call Martin Ames before noon on April 19 to confirm afternoon meeting with Bob Greenwood on April 20th.
  III. Set up meeting room at noon for 2:30 P.M. meeting on April 19th.
  IV. Ashley Stanton contact Bob Greenwood at 9:00 A.M. on April 20 and set up meeting for June 6 at 8:30 A.M.
  V. Carol Guiland contact Shelby Van Ness during afternoon of April 20 and set up meeting for June 6 at 10:00 A.M.
  VI. Call airline and reserve tickets on June 6 for Roger Epstein trip to Denver on July 8.
  VII. Meeting at 2:30 P.M. on April 19th.

32. A chronological file for all of the above information would be 32.____
    A. II, I, III, VII, V, IV, VI   B. III, VII, II, I, IV, V, VI
    C. III, VII, I, II, V, IV, VI   D. II, III, I, VII, IV, V, VI

33. A chronological file for the date of April 19th would be 33.____
    A. II, III, VII, I   B. II, III, I, VII   C. VII, I, III, II   D. III, VII, I, II

34. Add the following information to the file, and then create a chronological file   34.____
    for April 20th: VIII. April 20: 3:00 P.M. meeting between Bob Greenwood and
    Martin Ames.
    A. IV, V, VIII   B. IV, VIII, V   C. VIII, V, IV   D. V, IV, VIII

35. The PRIMARY advantage of computer records over a manual system is   35.____
    A. speed of retrieval   B. accuracy
    C. cost   D. potential file loss

KEY (CORRECT ANSWERS)

1. B	11. D	21. A	31. C
2. C	12. C	22. B	32. D
3. D	13. B	23. C	33. B
4. A	14. C	24. D	34. A
5. D	15. D	25. A	35. A
6. C	16. B	26. B	
7. B	17. C	27. C	
8. B	18. D	28. D	
9. C	19. A	29. A	
10. D	20. D	30. B	

CLERICAL ABILITIES TEST
EXAMINATION SECTION
TEST 1

DIRECTIONS: Each question or incomplete statement is followed by several suggested answers or completions. Select the one that BEST answers the question or completes the statement. *PRINT THE LETTER OF THE CORRECT ANSWER IN THE SPACE AT THE RIGHT.*

Questions 1-10.

DIRECTIONS: Questions 1 through 10 consist of lines of names, dates, and numbers. For each question, you are to choose the option (A, B, C, or D) in Column II which EXACTLY matches the information in Column I. *PRINT THE LETTER OF THE CORRECT ANSWER IN THE SPACE AT THE RIGHT.*

SAMPLE QUESTION

Column I
Schneider 11/16/75 581932

Column II
A. Schneider 11/16/75 518932
B. Schneider 11/16/75 581932
C. Schnieder 11/16/75 581932
D. Shnieder 11/16/75 518932

The correct answer is B. Only Option B shows the name, date, and number exactly as they are in Column I. Option A has a mistake in the number. Option C has a mistake in the name. Option D has a mistake in the name and in the number. Now answer Questions 1 through 10 in the same manner.

Column I
1. Johnston 12/26/74 659251

Column II
A. Johnson 12/23/74 659251
B. Johston 12/26/74 659251
C. Johnston 12/26/74 695251
D. Johnston 12/26/74 659251

1.____

2. Allison 1/26/75 9939256

A. Allison 1/26/75 9939256
B. Alisson 1/26/75 9939256
C. Allison 1/26/76 9399256
D. Allison 1/26/75 9993356

2.____

3. Farrell 2/12/75 361251

A. Farell 2/21/75 361251
B. Farrell 2/12/75 361251
C. Farrell 2/21/75 361251
D. Farrell 2/12/75 361151

3.____

4. Guerrero 4/28/72 105689
   A. Guererro 4/28/72 105689
   B. Guererro 4/28/72 105986
   C. Guererro 4/28/72 105869
   D. Guerrero 4/28/72 105689

   4._____

5. McDonnell 6/05/73 478215
   A. McDonnell 6/15/73 478215
   B. McDonnell 6/05/73 478215
   C. McDonnell 6/05/73 472815
   D. MacDonell 6/05/73 478215

   5._____

6. Shepard 3/31/71 075421
   A. Sheperd 3/31/71 075421
   B. Shepard 3/13/71 075421
   C. Shepard 3/31/71 075421
   D. Shepard 3/13/71 075241

   6._____

7. Russell 4/01/69 031429
   A. Russell 4/01/69 031429
   B. Russell 4/10/69 034129
   C. Russell 4/10/69 031429
   D. Russell 4/01/69 034129

   7._____

8. Phillips 10/16/68 961042
   A. Philipps 10/16/68 961042
   B. Phillips 10/16/68 960142
   C. Phillips 10/16/68 961042
   D. Philipps 10/16/68 916042

   8._____

9. Campbell 11/21/72 624856
   A. Campbell 11/21/72 624856
   B. Campbell 11/21/72 624586
   C. Campbell 11/21/72 624686
   D. Campbel 11/21/72 624856

   9._____

10. Patterson 9/18/71 76199176
    A. Patterson 9/18/72 76191976
    B. Patterson 9/18/71 76199176
    C. Patterson 9/18/72 76199176
    D. Patterson 9/18/71 76919176

    10._____

Questions 11-15.

DIRECTIONS: Questions 11 through 15 consist of groups of numbers and letters which you are to compare. For each question, you are to choose the option (A, B, C, or D) in Column I which EXACTLY matches the group of numbers and letters given in Column I.

SAMPLE QUESTION

Column I
B92466

Column II
A. B92644
B. B94266
C. A92466
D. B92466

The correct answer is D. Only Option D in Column II shows the group of numbers and letters EXACTLY as it appears in Column I. Now answer Questions 11 through 15 in the same manner.

	Column I	Column II	
11.	925AC5	A. 952CA5 B. 925AC5 C. 952AC5 D. 925CA6	11.____
12.	Y006925	A. Y060925 B. Y006295 C. Y006529 D. Y006925	12.____
13.	J236956	A. J236956 B. J326965 C. J239656 D. J932656	13.____
14.	AB6952	A. AB6952 B. AB9625 C. AB9652 D. AB6925	14.____
15.	X259361	A. X529361 B. X259631 C. X523961 D. X259361	15.____

Questions 16-25.

DIRECTIONS: Each of questions 16 through 25 consists of three lines of code letters and three lines of numbers. The numbers on each line should correspond with the code letters on the same line in accordance with the table below.

Code Letter	S	V	W	A	Q	M	X	E	G	K
Corresponding Number	0	1	2	3	4	5	5	7	8	9

On some of the lines, an error exists in the coding. Compare the letters and numbers in each question carefully. If you find an error or errors on:
    only one of the lines in the question, mark your answer A;
    any two lines in the question, mark your answer B;
    all three lines in the question, mark your answer C;
    none of the lines in the question, mark your answer D.

SAMPLE QUESTION

WQGKSXG   2489068
XEKVQMA   6591453
KMAESXV   9527061

In the above sample, the first line is correct since each code letter listed has the correct corresponding number. On the second line, an error exists because code letter E should have the number 7 instead of the number 5. On the third line, an error exists because the code letter A should have the number 3 instead of the number 2. Since there are errors in two of the three lines, the correct answer is B. Now answer Questions 16 through 25 in the same manner.

16. SWQEKGA   0247983   16.____
    KEAVSXM   9731065
    SSAXGKQ   0036894

17. QAMKMVS   4259510   17.____
    MGGEASX   5897306
    KSWMKWS   9125920

18. WKXQWVE   2964217   18.____
    QKXXQVA   4966413
    AWMXGVS   3253810

19. GMMKASE   8559307   19.____
    AWVSKSW   3210902
    QAVSVGK   4310189

20. XGKQSMK   6894049   20.____
    QSVKEAS   4019730
    GSMXKMV   8057951

21. AEKMWSG   3195208   21.____
    MKQSVQK   5940149
    XGQAEVW   6843712

22. XGMKAVS   6858310   22.____
    SKMAWEQ   0953174
    GVMEQSA   8167403

23. VQSKAVE   1489317   23.____
    WQGKAEM   2489375
    MEGKAWQ   5689324

24. XMQVSKG   6541098   24.____
    QMEKEWS   4579720
    KMEVGKG   9571983

5 (#1)

25. GKVAMEW   88912572   25._____
     AXMVKAE   3651937
     KWAGMAV   9238531

Questions 26-35.

DIRECTIONS: Each of Questions 26 through 35 consists of a column of figures. For each
question, add the column of figures and choose the correct answer from the
four choices given.

26. 5,665.43   26._____
     2,356.69
     6,447.24
     7,239.65

     A. 20,698.01   B. 21,709.01
     C. 21,718.01   D. 22,609.01

27. 817,209.55   27._____
     264,354.29
      82,368.76
     849,964.89

     A. 1,893.977.49   B. 1,989,988.39
     C. 2,009,077.39   D. 2,013,897.49

28. 156,366.89   28._____
     249,973.23
     823,229.49
      56,869.45

     A. 1,286,439.06   B. 1,287,521.06
     C. 1,297,539.06   D. 1,296,421.06

29.   23,422.15   29._____
     149,696.24
     238,377.53
      86,289.79
     505,533.63

     A. 989,229.34   B. 999,879.34
     C. 1,003,330.34   D. 1,023,329.34

95

30. 2,468,926.70
    656,842.28
    49,723.15
    832,369.59

    A. 3,218,062.72   B. 3,808,092.72
    C. 4,007,861.72   D. 4,818,192.72

    30. C

31.   524,201.52
    7,775,678.51
    8,345,299.63
    40,628,898.08
    31,374,670.07

    A. 88,646,647.81   B. 88,646,747.91
    C. 88,648,647.91   D. 88,648,747.81

    31. D

32. 6,824,829.40
      682,482.94
    5,542,015.27
      775,678.51
    7,732,507.25

    A. 21,557,513.37   B. 21,567,513.37
    C. 22,567,503.37   D. 22,567,513.37

    32. A

33. 22,109,405.58
     6,097,093.43
     5,050,073.99
     8,118,050.05
     4,313,980.82

    A. 45,688,593.87   B. 45,688,603.87
    C. 45,689,593.87   D. 45,689,603.87

    33. B

34. 79,324,114.19
    99,848,129.74
    43,331,653.31
    41,610,207.14

    A. 264,114,104.38   B. 264,114,114.38
    C. 265,114,114.38   D. 265,214,104.38

    34. A

35. 33,729,653.94
     5,959,342.58
     26,052,715.47
     4,452,669.52
     7,079,953.59

35.____

    A. 76,374,334.10   B. 76,375,334.10
    C. 77,274,335.10   D. 77,275,335.10

Questions 36-40.

DIRECTIONS: Each of Questions 36 through 40 consists of a single number in Column I and four options in Column II. For each question, you are to choose the option (A, B, C, or D) in Column II which EXACTLY matches the number in Column I.

SAMPLE QUESTION

Column I
5965121

Column II
A. 5956121
B. 5965121
C. 5966121
D. 5965211

The correct answer is B. Only Option B shows the number EXACTLY as it appears in Column I. Now answer Questions 36 through 40 in the same manner.

	Column I	Column II	
36.	9643242	A. 9643242 B. 9462342 C. 9642442 D. 9463242	36.____
37.	3572477	A. 3752477 B. 3725477 C. 3572477 D. 3574277	37.____
38.	5276101	A. 5267101 B. 5726011 C. 5271601 D. 5276101	38.____
39.	4469329	A. 4496329 B. 4469329 C. 4496239 D. 4469239	39.____

40. 2326308
A. 2236308
B. 2233608
C. 2326308
D. 2323608

40.____

KEY (CORRECT ANSWERS)

1.	D	11.	B	21.	A	31.	D
2.	A	12.	D	22.	C	32.	A
3.	B	13.	A	23.	B	33.	B
4.	D	14.	A	24.	D	34.	A
5.	B	15.	D	25.	A	35.	C
6.	C	16.	D	26.	B	36.	A
7.	A	17.	C	27.	D	37.	C
8.	C	18.	A	28.	A	38.	D
9.	A	19.	D	29.	C	39.	B
10.	B	20.	B	30.	C	40.	C

TEST 2

DIRECTIONS: Each question or incomplete statement is followed by several suggested answers or completions. Select the one that BEST answers the question or completes the statement. *PRINT THE LETTER OF THE CORRECT ANSWER IN THE SPACE AT THE RIGHT.*

Questions 1-5.

DIRECTIONS: Each of Questions 1 through 5 consists of a name and a dollar amount. In each question, the name and dollar amount in Column II should be an EXACT copy of the name and dollar amount in Column I. If there is:
    a mistake only in the name, mark your answer A;
    a mistake only in the dollar amount, mark your answer B;
    a mistake in both the name and the dollar amount, mark your answer C;
    no mistake in either the name or the dollar amount, mark your answer D.

SAMPLE QUESTION

Column I	Column II
George Peterson	George Petersson
$125.50	$125.50

Compare the name and dollar amount in Column II with the name and dollar amount in Column I. The name *Petersson* in Column II is spelled *Peterson* in Column I. The amount is the same in both columns. Since there is a mistake only in the name, the answer to the sample question is A. Now answer Questions 1 through 5 in the same manner.

	Column I	Column II	
1.	Susanne Shultz $3440	Susanne Schultz $3440	1.____
2.	Anibal P. Contrucci $2121.61	Anibel P. Contrucci $2112.61	2.____
3.	Eugenio Mendoza $12.45	Eugenio Mendozza $12.45	3.____
4.	Maurice Gluckstadt $4297	Maurice Gluckstadt $4297	4.____
5.	John Pampellonne $4656.94	John Pammpellonne $4566.94	5.____

Questions 6-11.

DIRECTIONS: Each of Questions 6 through 11 consist of a set of names and addresses, which you are to compare. In each question, the name and addresses in Column II should be an EXACT copy of the name and address in Column I. If there is:
- a mistake only in the name, mark your answer A;
- a mistake only in the address, mark your answer B;
- a mistake in both the name and address, mark your answer C;
- no mistake in either the name or address, mark your answer D.

SAMPLE QUESTION

Column I
Michael Filbert
456 Reade Street
New York, N.Y. 10013

Column II
Michael Filbert
645 Reade Street
New York, N.Y. 10013

Since there is a mistake only in the address (the street number should be 456 instead of 645), the answer to the sample question is B. Now answer Questions 6 through 11 in the same manner.

Column I

6. Hilda Goettelmann
   55 Lenox Rd.
   Brooklyn, N.Y. 11226

7. Arthur Sherman
   2522 Batchelder St.
   Brooklyn, N.Y. 11235

8. Ralph Barnett
   300 West 28 Street
   New York, New York 10001

9. George Goodwin
   135 Palmer Avenue
   Staten Island, New York 10302

10. Alonso Ramirez
    232 West 79 Street
    New York, N.Y. 10024

11. Cynthia Graham
    149-34 83 Street
    Howard Beach, N.Y. 11414

Column II

6. Hilda Goettelman
   55 Lenox Ave.
   Brooklyn, N.Y. 11226

7. Arthur Sharman
   2522 Batcheder St.
   Brooklyn, N.Y. 11253

8. Ralph Barnett
   300 West 28 Street
   New York, New York 10001

9. George Godwin
   135 Palmer Avenue
   Staten Island, New York 10302

10. Alonso Ramirez
    223 West 79 Street
    New York, N.Y. 10024

11. Cynthia Graham
    149-35 83 Street
    Howard Beach, N.Y. 11414

6. ____
7. ____
8. ____
9. ____
10. ____
11. ____

Questions 12-20.

DIRECTIONS: Questions 12 through 20 are problems in subtraction. For each question do the subtraction and select your answer from the four choices given.

12. 232,921.85
    -179,587.68

    A. 52,433.17
    C. 53,334.17
    B. 52,434.17
    D. 53,343,17

12.____

13. 5,531,876.29
    -3,897,158.36

    A. 1,634,717.93
    C. 1,734,717.93
    B. 1,644,718.93
    D. 1,7234,718.93

13.____

14. 1,482,658.22
    -937,925.76

    A. 544,633.46
    C. 545,632.46
    B. 544,732.46
    D. 545,732.46

14.____

15. 937,828.17
    -259,673.88

    A. 678,154.29
    C. 688,155.39
    B. 679,154.29
    D. 699,155.39

15.____

16. 760,412.38
    -263,465.95

    A. 496,046.43
    C. 496,956.43
    B. 496,946.43
    D. 497,046.43

16.____

17. 3,203,902.26
    -2,933,087.96

    A. 260,814.30
    C. 270,814.30
    B. 269,824.30
    D. 270,824.30

17.____

18. 1,023,468.71
    -934,678.88

    A. 88,780.83
    C. 88,880.83
    B. 88,789.83
    D. 88,889.83

18.____

19. 831,549.47
    -772,814.78

    A. 58,734.69   B. 58,834.69
    C. 59,735.69   D. 59,834.69

20. 6,306,181.74
    -3,617,376.99

    A. 2,687,904.99   B. 2,688,904.99
    C. 2,689,804.99   D. 2,799,905.99

Questions 21-30.

DIRECTIONS: Each of Questions 21 through 30 consists of three lines of code letters and three lines of numbers. The numbers on each line should correspond with the code letters on the same line in accordance with the table below.

Code Letter	J	U	B	T	Y	D	K	R	L	P
Corresponding Number	0	1	2	3	4	5	5	7	8	9

On some of the lines, an error exists in the coding. Compare the letters and numbers in each question carefully. If you find an error or errors on:
only *one* of the lines in the question, mark your answer A;
any *two* lines in the question, mark your answer B;
all *three* lines in the question, mark your answer C;
none of the lines in the question, mark your answer D.

SAMPLE QUESTION

BJRPYUR   2079417
DTBPYKJ   5328460
YKLDBLT   4685283

In the above sample, the first line is correct since each code letter listed has the correct corresponding number. On the second line, an error exists because code letter P should have the number 9 instead of the number 8. The third line is correct since each code letter listed has the correct corresponding number. Since there is an error in *one* of the three lines, the correct answer is A. Now answer Questions 21 through 30 in the same manner.

21. BYPDTJL   2495308
    PLRDTJU   9815301
    DTJRYLK   5207486

22. RPBYRJK   7934706
    PKTYLBU   9624821
    KDLPJYR   6489047

23.	TPYBUJR	3942107	23._____
	BYRKPTU	2476931	
	DUKPYDL	5169458	
24.	KBYDLPL	6345898	24._____
	BLRKBRU	2876261	
	JTULDYB	0318542	
25.	LDPYDKR	8594567	25._____
	BDKDRJL	2565708	
	BDRPLUJ	2679810	
26.	PLRLBPU	9858291	26._____
	LPYKRDJ	88936750	
	TDKPDTR	3569527	
27.	RKURPBY	7617924	27._____
	RYUKPTJ	7426930	
	RTKPTJD	7369305	
28.	DYKPBJT	5469203	28._____
	KLPJBTL	6890238	
	TKPLBJP	3698209	
29.	BTPRJYL	2397148	29._____
	LDKUTYR	8561347	
	YDBLRPJ	4528190	
30.	ULPBKYT	1892643	30._____
	KPDTRBJ	6953720	
	YLKJPTB	4860932	

KEY (CORRECT ANSWERS)

1.	A	11.	D	21.	B
2.	C	12.	C	22.	C
3.	A	13.	A	23.	D
4.	D	14.	B	24.	B
5.	C	15.	A	25.	A
6.	C	16.	B	26.	C
7.	C	17.	C	27.	A
8.	D	18.	B	28.	D
9.	A	19.	A	29.	B
10.	B	20.	B	30.	D

NAME AND NUMBER CHECKING
EXAMINATION SECTION
TEST 1

DIRECTIONS: This test is designed to measure your speed/and accuracy. You are urged to work both quickly and accurately and to do correctly as many lists as you can in the time allowed. The test consists of lists or pairs of names and numbers. Count the number of IDENTICAL pairs in each list. Then, select the correct number, 1, 2, 3, 4, 5, and indicate your choice in the space at the right. Two sample questions are presented for your guidance, together with the correct solutions.

SAMPLE LIST A
Adelphi College – Adelphia College
Braxton Corp – Braxeton Corp.
Wassaic State School – Wassaic State School
Central Islip State Hospital – Central Isllip State Hospital
Greenwich House – Greenwich House

NOTE: There are only two correct pairs—Wassaic State School and Greenwich House. Therefore, the CORRECT answer is 2.

SAMPLE LIST B
78453694 – 78453684
784530 – 784530
533 – 534
67845 – 67845
2368745 – 2368755

NOTE: There are only two correct pairs—784530 and 67845. Therefore, the CORRECT answer is 2.

LIST 1   1.____
    Diagnostic Clinic   – Diagnostic Clinic
    Yorkville Health   – Yorkville Health
    Meinhard Clinic   – Meinhart Clinic
    Corlears Clinic   – Carlears Clinic
    Tremont Diagnostic – Tremont Diagnostic

LIST 2   2.____
    73526   – 73526
    7283627198   – 7283627198
    627   – 637
    728352617283 – 7283526178282
    6281   – 6281

LIST 3
    Jefferson Clinic   – Jeffersen Clinic
    Mott Haven Center   – Mott Havan Center
    Bronx Hospital   – Bronx Hospital
    Montefiore Hospital   – Montifeore Hospital
    Beth Isreal Hospital   – Beth Israel Hospital

3.____

LIST 4
    936271826   – 936371826
    5271   – 5291
    82637192037   – 82637192037
    527182   – 5271882
    726354256   - 72635456

4.____

LIST 5
    Trinity Hospital   – Trinity Hospital
    Central Harlem   – Centrel Harlem
    St. Luke's Hospital   – St. Lukes' Hospital
    Mt. Sinai Hospital   – Mt. Sinia Hospital
    N.Y. Dispensery   – N.Y. Dispensary

5.____

LIST 6
    725361552637   – 725361555637
    7526378   – 7526377
    6975   – 6975
    82637481028   – 82637481028
    3427   – 3429

6.____

LIST 7
    Misericordia Hospital   – Miseracordia Hospital
    Lebonan Hospital   – Lebanon Hospital
    Gouverneur Hospital   – Gouverner Hospital
    German Polyclinic   – German Policlinic
    French Hospital   – French Hospital

7.____

LIST 8
    8277364933251   – 827364933351
    63728   – 63728
    367281   – 367281
    62733846273   – 6273846293
    62836   - 6283

8.____

LIST 9
    King's County Hospital   – Kings County Hospital
    St. Johns Long Island   – St. John's Long Island
    Bellevue Hospital   – Bellvue Hospital
    Beth David Hospital   – Beth David Hospital
    Samaritan Hospital   – Samariton Hospital

9.____

3 (#1)

LIST 10   10._____
   62836454   – 62836455
   42738267   – 42738369
   573829   – 573829
   738291627874   – 738291627874
   725   - 735

LIST 11   11._____
   Bloomingdal Clinic   – Bloomingdale Clinic
   Communitty Hospital – Community Hospital
   Metroplitan Hospital – Metropoliton Hospital
   Lenox Hill Hospital   – Lonex Hill Hospital
   Lincoln Hospital   – Lincoln Hospital

LIST 12   12._____
   6283364728   – 6283648
   627385   – 627383
   54283902   – 54283602
   63354   – 63354
   7283562781   - 7283562781

LIST 13   13._____
   Sydenham Hospital   – Sydanham Hospital
   Roosevalt Hospital   – Roosevelt Hospital
   Vanderbilt Clinic   – Vanderbild Clinic
   Women's Hospital   – Woman's Hospital
   Flushing Hospital   – Flushing Hospital

LIST 14   14._____
   62738   – 62738
   727355542321   – 72735542321
   263849332   – 263849332
   262837   – 263837
   47382912   - 47382922

LIST 15   15._____
   Episcopal Hospital   – Episcapal Hospital
   Flower Hospital   – Flouer Hospital
   Stuyvesent Clinic   – Stuyvesant Clinic
   Jamaica Clinic   – Jamaica Clinic
   Ridgwood Clinic   – Ridgewood Clinic

LIST 16   16._____
   628367299   – 628367399
   111   – 111
   118293304829   – 1182839489
   4448   – 4448
   333693678   - 333693678

4 (#1)

LIST 17   17.____
    Arietta Crane Farm   – Areitta Crane Farm
    Bikur Chilim Home   – Bikur Chilom Home
    Burke Foundation   – Burke Foundation
    Blythedale Home   – Blythdale Home
    Campbell Cottages   – Cambell Cottages

LIST 18   18.____
    32123   – 32132
    273893326783   – 27389326783
    473829   – 473829
    7382937   – 7383937
    3628890122332   - 36289012332

LIST 19   19.____
    Caraline Rest   – Caroline Rest
    Loreto Rest   – Loretto Rest
    Edgewater Creche   – Edgwater Creche
    Holiday Farm   – Holiday Farm
    House of St. Giles   – House of st. Giles

LIST 20   20.____
    557286777   – 55728677
    3678902   – 3678892
    1567839   – 1567839
    7865434712   – 7865344712
    9927382   - 9927382

LIST 21   21.____
    Isabella Home   – Isabela Home
    James A. Moore Home   – James A. More Home
    The Robin's Nest   – The Roben's Nest
    Pelham Home   – Pelam Home
    St. Eleanora's Home   – St. Eleanora's Home

LIST 22   22.____
    273648293048   – 273648293048
    334   – 334
    7362536478   – 7362536478
    7362819273   – 7362819273
    7362   - 7363

LIST 23   23.____
    St. Pheobe's Mission   – St. Phebe's Mission
    Seaside Home   – Seaside Home
    Speedwell Society   – Speedwell Society
    Valeria Home   – Valera Home
    Wiltwyck   - Wildwyck

5 (#1)

LIST 24
    63728   – 63738
    63728192736   – 63728192738
    428   – 458
    62738291527   – 62738291529
    63728192   - 63728192

24.____

LIST 25
    McGaffin   – McGafin
    David Ardslee   – David Ardslee
    Axton Supply   – Axeton Supply Co
    Alice Russell   – Alice Russell
    Dobson Mfg. Co.   – Dobsen Mfg. Co.

25.____

KEY (CORRECT ANSWERS)

1.	3		11.	1
2.	3		12.	2
3.	1		13.	1
4.	1		14.	2
5.	1		15.	1
6.	2		16.	3
7.	1		17.	1
8.	2		18.	1
9.	1		19.	1
10.	2		20.	2

21.	1
22.	4
23.	2
24.	1
25.	2

TEST 2

DIRECTIONS: This test is designed to measure your speed/and accuracy. You are urged to work both quickly and accurately and to do correctly as many lists as you can in the time allowed. The test consists of lists or pairs of names and numbers. Count the number of IDENTICAL pairs in each list. Then, select the correct number, 1, 2, 3, 4, 5, and indicate your choice in the space at the right.

LIST 1   1._____
     82637381028   – 82637281028
     928   – 928
     72937281028   – 72937281028
     7362   – 7362
     927382615   – 927382615

LIST 2   2._____
     Albee Theatre   – Albee Theatre
     Lapland Lumber Co.   – Laplund Lumber Co.
     Adelphi College   – Adelphi College
     Jones & Son Inc.   – Jones & Sons Inc.
     S.W. Ponds Co.   – S.W. Ponds Co.

LIST 3   3._____
     85345   – 85345
     895643278   – 895643277
     726352   – 726353
     632685   – 632685
     7263524   – 7236524

LIST 4   4._____
     Eagle Library   – Eagle Library
     Dodge Ltd.   – Dodge Co.
     Stromberg Carlson   – Stromberg Carlsen
     Clairice Ling   – Clairice Linng
     Mason Book Co.   – Matson Book Co.

LIST 5   5._____
     66273   – 66273
     629   – 629
     7382517283   – 7382517283
     637281   – 639281
     2738261   – 2788261

LIST 6   6._____
     Robert MacColl   – Robert McColl
     Buick Motor   – Buck Motors
     Murray Bay & Co. Ltd.   – Murray Bay Co. Ltd.
     L.T. Ltyle   – L.T. Lyttle
     A.S. Landas   – A.S. Landas

LIST 7
- 6271526374890 — 627152637490
- 73526189 — 73526189
- 5372 — 5392
- 637281142 — 63728124
- 4783946 — 4783046

7.____

LIST 8
- Tyndall Burke — Tyndell Burke
- W. Briehl — W. Briehl
- Burritt Publishing Co. — Buritt Publishing Co.
- Frederick Breyer & Co. — Frederick Breyer Co.
- Bailey Buulard — Bailey Bullard

8.____

LIST 9
- 634 — 634
- 16837 — 163837
- 273892223678 — 27389223678
- 527182 — 527782
- 3628901223 — 3629002223

9.____

LIST 10
- Ernest Boas — Ernest Boas
- Rankin Barne — Rankin Barnes
- Edward Appley — Edward Appely
- Camel — Camel
- Caiger Food Co. — Caiger Food Co.

10.____

LIST 11
- 6273 — 6273
- 322 — 332
- 15672839 — 15672839
- 63728192637 — 63728192639
- 738 — 738

11.____

LIST 12
- Wells Fargo Co. — Wells Fargo Co.
- W.D. Brett — W.D. Britt
- Tassco Co. — Tassko Co.
- Republic Mills — Republic Mill
- R.W. Burnham — R.W. Burhnam

12.____

LIST 13
- 7253529152 — 7283529152
- 6283 — 6383
- 52839102738 — 5283910238
- 308 — 398
- 82637201927 — 8263720127

13.____

LIST 14
    Schumacker Co.   – Shumacker Co.
    C.H. Caiger   – C.H. Caiger
    Abraham Strauss   – Abram Straus
    B.F. Boettjer   – B.F. Boettijer
    Cut-Rate Store   – Cut-Rate Stores

14.____

LIST 15
    15273826   – 15273826
    72537   – 73537
    726391027384   – 62639107384
    637389   – 627399
    725382910   – 725382910

15.____

LIST 16
    Hixby Ltd.   – Hixby Lt'd.
    S. Reiner   – S. Riener
    Reynard Co.   – Reynord Co.
    Esso Gassoline Co.   – Esso Gasolene Co.
    Belle Brock   – Belle Brock

16.____

LIST 17
    7245   – 7245
    819263728192   – 819263728172
    682537289   – 682537298
    789   – 789
    82936542891   – 82936542891

17.____

LIST 18
    Joseph Cartwright   – Joseph Cartwrite
    Foote Food Co.   – Foot Food Co.
    Weiman & Held   – Weiman & Held
    Sanderson Shoe Co.   – Sandersen Shoe Co.
    A.M. Byrne   – A.N. Byrne

18.____

LIST 19
    4738267   – 4738277
    63728   – 63729
    6283628901   – 6283628991
    918264   – 918264
    263728192037   – 2637728192073

19.____

LIST 20
    Exray Laboratories   – Exray Labratories
    Curley Toy Co.   – Curly Toy Co.
    J. Lauer & Cross   – J. Laeur & Cross
    Mireco Brands   – Mireco Brands
    Sandor Lorand   – Sandor Larand

20.____

4 (#2)

LIST 21   21.____
- 607 — 609
- 6405 — 6403
- 976 — 996
- 101267 — 101267
- 2065432 — 20965432

LIST 22   22.____
- John Macy & Sons — John Macy & Son
- Venus Pencil Co. — Venus Pencil Co.
- Nell McGinnis — Nell McGinnis
- McCutcheon & Co. — McCutcheon & Co.
- Sun-Tan Oil — Sun-Tan Oil

LIST 23   23.____
- 703345700 — 703345700
- 46754 — 466754
- 3367490 — 3367490
- 3379 — 3778
- 47384 — 47394

LIST 24   24.____
- arthritis — arthritis
- asthma — asthma
- endocrine — endocrene
- gastro-enterological — gastrol-enteralogical
- orthopedic — orthopedic

LIST 25   25.____
- 743829432 — 743828432
- 998 — 998
- 732816253902 — 732816252902
- 46829 — 46830
- 7439120249 — 7439210249

KEY (CORRECT ANSWERS)

1.	4	11.	3
2.	3	12.	1
3.	2	13.	1
4.	1	14.	1
5.	2	15.	2
6.	1	16.	1
7.	2	17.	3
8.	1	18.	1
9.	1	19.	1
10.	3	20.	1

21. 1
22. 4
23. 2
24. 3
25. 1

ARITHMETIC
EXAMINATION SECTION
TEST 1

DIRECTIONS: Each question or incomplete statement is followed by several suggested answers or completions. Select the one that BEST answers the question or completes the statement. PRINT THE LETTER OF TEE CORRECT ANSWER IN THE SPACE AT THE RIGHT.

1. Add $4.34, $34.50, $6.00, $101.76, $90.67. From the result, subtract $60.54 and $10,56.   1.____
   A. $76.17   B. $156.37   C. $166.17   D. $300.37

2. Add 2,200, 2,600, 252 and 47.96. From the result, subtract 202.70, 1,200, 2,150 and 434.43.   2.____
   A. 1,112.83   B. 1,213.46   C. 1,341.51   D. 1,348.91

3. Multiply 1850 by .05 and multiply 3300 by .08 and, then, add both results,   3.____
   A. 242.50   B. 264,00   C. 333.25   D. 356.50

4. Multiply 312.77 by .04. Round off the result to the nearest hundredth.   4.____
   A. 12.52   B. 12.511   C. 12.518   D. 12.51

5. Add 362.05, 91.13, 347.81 and 17.46 and then divide the result by 6. The answer, rounded off to the nearest hundredth, is: 5.____
   A. 138.409   B. 137.409   C. 136.41   D. 136.40

6. Add 66.25 and 15.06 and, then, multiply the result by 2 1/6. The answer is, most nearly,   6.____
   A. 176.18   B. 176.17   C. 162.66   D. 162.62

7. Each of the following items contains three decimals. In which case do all three decimals have the SAME value?   7.____
   A. .3; .30; .03   B. .25; .250; .2500
   C. 1.9; 1.90;1.09   D. .35; .350; .035

8. Add 1/2 the sum of (539.84 and 479.26) to 1/3 the sum of (1461.93 and 927.27). Round off the result to the nearest whole number.   8.____
   A. 3408   B. 2899   C. 1816   D. 1306

9. Multiply $5,906.09 by 15% and, then, divide the result by 3 and round off to the nearest cent.   9.____
   A. $295.30   B. $885.91   C. $2,657.74   D. $29,530.45

10. Multiply 630 by 517.   10.____
    A. 325,710   B. 345,720   C. 362,425   D. 385,660

115

11. Multiply 35 by 846.   11._____
    A. 4050   B. 9450   C. 18740   D. 29610

12. Multiply 823 by 0.05.   12._____
    A. 0.4115   B. 4.115   C. 41.15   D. 411.50

13. Multiply 1690 by 0.10.   13._____
    A. 0.169   B. .1.69   C. 16.90   D. 169.0

14. Divide 2765 by 35.   14._____
    A. 71   B. 79   C. 87   D. 93

15. From $18.55 subtract $6.80.   15._____
    A. $9.75   B. $10.95   C. $11.75   D. $25.35

16. The sum of 2.75 + 4.50 + 3.60 is: 16._____
    A. 9.75   B. 10.85   C. 11.15   D. 11.95

17. The sum of 9.63 + 11.21 + 17.25 is: 17._____
    A. 36.09   B. 38.09   C. 39.92   D. 41.22

18. The sum of 112.0 + 16.9 + 3.84 is: 18._____
    A. 129.3   B. 132.74   C. 136.48   D. 167.3

19. When 65 is added to the result of 14 multiplied by 13, the answer is: 19._____
    A. 92   B. 182   C. 247   D. 16055

20. From $391.55 subtract $273.45.   20._____
    A. $118.10   B. $128.20   C. $178.10   D. $218.20

KEY (CORRECT ANSWERS)

1.	C	11.	D
2.	A	12.	C
3.	D	13.	D
4.	D	14.	B
5.	C	15.	C
6.	B	16.	B
7.	B	17.	B
8.	D	18.	B
9.	C	19.	C
10.	A	20.	A

SOLUTIONS TO PROBLEMS

1. ($4.34 + $34.50 + $6.00 + $101.76 + $90.67) - ($60.54 + $10.56) = $237.27 - $71.10 = $166.17.

2. (2200 + 2600 + 252 + 47.96) - (202.70 + 1200 + 2150 + 434.43) = 5099.96 - 3987.13 = 1112.83

3. (1850)(.05) + (3300)(.08) = 92.5 + 264 = 356.50

4. (312.77)(.04) = 12.5108 = 12.51 to nearest hundredth

5. $(362.05 + 91.13 + 347.81 + 17.46) \div 6 = 136.408\overline{3} = 136.41$ to nearest hundredth

6. $(66.25 + 15.06)(2\frac{1}{6}) = 176.171\overline{6} \approx 176.17$

7. .25 = .250 = .2500

8. $(\frac{1}{2})(539.84 + 479.26) + \frac{1}{3}(1461.93 + 927.27) = 509.55 + 796.4 = 1305.95 = 1306$ nearest whole number

9. ($5906.09)(.15) ÷ 3 = ($885.9135)/3 = 295.3045 = $295.30 to nearest cent

10. (630)(517) = 325,710

11. (35)(846) = 29,610

12. (823)(.05) = 41.15

13. (1690)(10) = 169.0

14. 2765 ÷ 3.5 = 79

15. $18.55 - $6.80 = $11.75

16. 2.75 + 4.50 + 3.60 = 10.85

17. 9.63 + 11.21 + 17.25 = 38.09

18. 112.0 + 16.9 + 3.84 = 132.74

19. 65 + (14)(13) = 65 + 182 = 247

20. $391.55 - $273.45 = $118.10

TEST 2

DIRECTIONS: Each question or incomplete statement is followed by several suggested answers or completions. Select the one that BEST answers the question or completes the statement. PRINT THE LETTER OF TEE CORRECT ANSWER IN THE SPACE AT THE RIGHT.

1. The sum of $29.61 + $101.53 + $943.64 is: 1._____
   A. $983.88   B. $1074.78   C. $1174.98   D. $1341.42

2. The sum of $132.25 + $85.63 + $7056,44 is: 2._____
   A. $1694.19   B. $7274.32   C. $8464.57   D. $9346.22

3. The sum of 4010 + 1271 + 838 + 23 is: 3._____
   A. 6142   B. 6162   C. 6242   D. 6362

4. The sum of 53632 + 27403 + 98765 + 75424 is: 4._____
   A. 19214   B. 215214   C. 235224   D. 255224

5. The sum of 76342 + 49050 + 21206 + 59989 is: 5._____
   A. 196586   B. 206087   C. 206587   D. 234487

6. The sum of $452.13 + $963.45 + $621.25 is: 6._____
   A. $1936.83   B. $2036.83   C. $2095.73   D. $2135.73

7. The sum of 36392 + 42156 + 98765 is: 7._____
   A. 167214   B. 177203   C. 177313   D. 178213

8. The sum of 40125 + 87123 + 24689 is: 8._____
   A. 141827   B. 151827   C. 151937   D. 161947

9. The sum of 2379 + 4015 + 6521 + 9986 is: 9._____
   A. 22901   B. 22819   C. 21801   D. 21791

10. From 50962 subtract 36197.   10._____
    A. 14675   B. 14765   C. 14865   D. 24765

11. From 90000 subtract 31928.   11._____
    A. 58072   B. 59062   C. 68172   D. 69182

12. From 63764 subtract 21548.   12._____
    A. 42216   B. 43122   C. 45126   D. 85312

13. From $9605.13 subtract $2715.96.   13._____
    A. $12,321.09   B. $8,690.16   C. $6,990.07   D. $6,889.17

14. From 76421 subtract 73101. 14.____
    A. 3642   B. 3540   C. 3320   D. 3242

15. From $8.25 subtract $6.50. 15.____
    A. $1.25   B. $1.50   C. $1.75   D. $2.25

16. Multiply 583 by 0.50. 16.____
    A. $291.50   B. 28.15   C. 2.815   D. 0.2815

17. Multiply 0.35 by 1045. 17.____
    A. 0.36575   B. 3.6575   C. 36.575   D. 365.75

18. Multiply 25 by 2513. 18.____
    A. 62825   B. 62725   C. 60825   D. 52825

19. Multiply 423 by 0.01. 19.____
    A. 0.0423   B. 0.423   C. 4.23   D. 42.3

20. Multiply 6.70 by 3.2. 20.____
    A. 2.1440   B. 21.440   C. 214.40   D. 2144.0

KEY (CORRECT ANSWERS)

1. B   11. A
2. B   12. A
3. A   13. D
4. D   14. C
5. C   15. C

6. B   16. A
7. C   17. D
8. C   18. A
9. A   19. C
10. B   20. B

SOLUTIONS TO PROBLEMS

1. $29.61 + $101.53 + $943.64 = $1074.78

2. $132.25 + $85.63 + $7056.44 = $7274.32

3. 4010 + 1271 + 838 + 23 = 6142

4. 53,632 + 27,403 + 98,765 + 75,424 = 255,224

5. 76,342 + 49,050 + 21,206 + 59,989 = 206,587

6. $452.13 + $963.45 + $621.25 = $2036.83

7. 36,392 + 42,156 + 98,765 = 177,313

8. 40,125 + 87,123 + 24,689 = 151,937

9. 2379 + 4015 + 6521 + 9986 = 22,901

10. 50962 - 36197 = 14,765

11. 90,000 - 31,928 = 58,072

12. 63,764 - 21,548 = 42,216

13. $9605.13 - $2715.96 = $6889.17

14. 76,421 - 73,101 = 3320

15. $8.25 - $6.50 = $1.75

16. (583)(.50) = 291.50

17. (.35)(1045) = 365.75

18. (25)(2513) = 62,825

19. (423)(.01) = 4.23

20. (6.70)(3.2) = 21.44

TEST 3

DIRECTIONS: Each question or incomplete statement is followed by several suggested answers or completions. Select the one that BEST answers the question or completes the statement. PRINT THE LETTER OF TEE CORRECT ANSWER IN THE SPACE AT THE RIGHT.

Questions 1-4.

DIRECTIONS: For each of Questions 1-4, perform the indicated arithmetic and choose the correct answer from among the four choices given.

1. 12.485
   + 347

   A. 12,038   B. 12,128   C. 12,782   D. 12,832

2. 74,137
   + 711

   A. 74,326   B. 74,848   C. 78,028   D. .D. 78,926

3. 3,749
   - 671

   A. 3,078   B. 3,168   C. 4,028   D. 4,420

4. 19,805
   -18904

   A. 109   B. 901   C. 1,109   D. 1,901

5. When 119 is subtracted from the sum of 2016 + 1634, the remainder is:

   A. 2460   B. 3531   C. 3650   D. 3769

6. Multiply 35 X 65 X 15.

   A. 2275   B. 24265   C. 31145   D. 34125

7. 90% expressed as a decimal is:

   A. .009   B. .09   C. .9   D. 9.0

8. Seven-tenths of a foot expressed in inches is:

   A. 5.5   B. 6.5   C. 7   D. 8.4

9. If 95 men were divided into crews of five men each, the *number* of crews that will be formed is:

   A. 16   B. 17   C. 18   D. 19

10. If a man earns $19.50 an hour, the *number* of working hours it will take him to earn $4,875 is, most nearly,

    A. 225   B. 250   C. 275   D. 300

11. If 5 1/2 loads of gravel cost $55.00, then 6 1/2 loads will cost:

    A. $60.   B. $62.50   C. $65.   D. $66.00

12. At $2.50 a yard, 27 yards of concrete will cost:

    A. $36.   B. $41.80   C. $54.   D. $67.50

13. A distance is measured and found to be 52.23 feet. In feet and inches, this distance is, most nearly, 52 feet *and*

    A. 2 3/4"   B. 3 1/4"   C. 3 3/4"   D. 4 1/4"

14. If a maintainer gets $5.20 per hour and time and one-half for working over 40 hours, his *gross* salary for a week in which he worked 43 hours would be

    A. $208.00   B. $223.60   C. $231.40   D. $335.40

15. The circumference of a circle is given by the formula $C = \Pi D$, where C is the circumference, D is the diameter, and Π is about 3 1/7.
    If a coil is 15 turns of steel cable has an average diameter of 20 inches, the *total* length of cable on the coil is *nearest to*

    A. 5 feet   B. 78 feet   C. 550 feet   D. 943 feet

16. The measurements of a poured concrete foundation show that 54 cubic feet of concrete have been placed.
    If payment for this concrete is to be on the basis of cubic yards, the 54 cubic feet must be

    A. multiplied by 27   B. multiplied by 3
    C. divided by 27   D. divided by 3

17. If the cost of 4 1/2 tons of structural steel is $1,800, then the cost of 12 tons is, most nearly,

    A. $4,800   B. $5,400   C. $7,200   D. $216,000

18. An hourly-paid employee working 12:00 midnight to 8:00 a.m. is directed to report to the medical staff for a physical examination at 11:00 a.m. of the same day.
    The pay allowed him for reporting will be an extra

    A. 1 hour   B. 2 hours   C. 3 hours   D. 4 hours

19. The *total* length of four pieces of 2" pipe, whose lengths are 7' 3 1/2", 4' 2 3/16", 5' 7 5/16", and 8' 5 7/8", respectively, is:

    A. 24' 6 3/4"   B. 24' 7 15/16"
    C. 25' 5 13/16"   D. 25' 6 7/8"

20. As a senior mortuary caretaker, you are preparing a monthly report, using the following figures: 20.____

    No. of bodies received   983
    No. of bodies claimed   720
    No. of bodies sent to city cemetery   14
    No. of bodies sent to medical schools   9

How many bodies remained at the end of the monthly reporting period?

    A. 230   B. 240   C. 250   D. 260

KEY (CORRECT ANSWERS)

1.	D	11.	C
2.	B	12.	D
3.	A	13.	A
4.	B	14.	C
5.	B	15.	B
6.	D	16.	C
7.	C	17.	A
8.	D	18.	C
9.	D	19.	D
10.	B	20.	B

SOLUTIONS TO PROBLEMS

1. 12,485 + 347 = 12,832

2. 74,137 + 711 = 74,848

3. 3749 - 671 = 3078

4. 19,805 - 18,904 = 901

5. (2016 + 1634) - 119 = 3650 - 119 = 3531

6. (35)(65)(15) = 34,125

7. 90% = .90 or .9

8. $(\frac{7}{10})(12) = 8.4$ inches

9. 95 ÷ 5 = 19 crews

10. $4875 ÷ $19.50 = 250 days

11. Let x = cost. Then, $\frac{5\frac{1}{2}}{6\frac{1}{2}} = \frac{\$55.00}{x}$. $5\frac{1}{2} = 357.50$. Solving, x = $65

12. ($2.50)(27) = $67.50

13. .23-ft. = 2.76 in., so 52.23 ft ≈ 52 ft. $2\frac{3}{4}$ in. (.76 ≈ $\frac{3}{4}$)

14. Salary = ($5.20)(40) + ($7.80)(3) = $231.40

15. Length ≈ (15)($3\frac{1}{7}$)(20) ≈ 943 in. ≈ 78 ft.

16. There are 27 cu.ft. in 1 cu.yd. To change from 54 cu.ft. to cu.yds., divide by 27.

17. $1800 ÷ $4\frac{1}{2}$ = = $400 per ton. Then, 12 tons cost ($400)(12) = $4800

18. Instead of working 12 to 8, he will be staying until 11 AM, an extra 3 hours.

19. 7'$3\frac{1}{2}$" + 4'$2\frac{3}{16}$" + 5'$7\frac{5}{16}$" + 8'$5\frac{7}{8}$" = 24'$17\frac{30}{16}$" = 24'$18\frac{7}{8}$"

20. 983 - 720 - 14 - 9 = 240 bodies left.

www.ingramcontent.com/pod-product-compliance
Lightning Source LLC
Chambersburg PA
CBHW082209300426

44117CB00016B/2731